Chasing Perfect strikes at the core of today's hustle culture, exposing the lies we've believed about our value, our work, and our purpose. In a necessary reorientation of heart and priority, Alisha directs us back to the only source of fulfillment—the Maker of our souls. This book shows the way to peace is found not by neglecting our full plates but by surrendering them to Christ.

—**Phylicia Masonheimer**, author | speaker | teacher, Driven Women

In a day when being busy and overwhelmed is the mark of a successful life, *Chasing Perfect* offers an important perspective shift: If we are looking to our achievements and performance to validate our worth, we will never be satisfied. This book will help you discover how to reprioritize your life to find lasting fulfillment in the pursuit of God, not perfection.

—**Lisa Bevere**, *New York Times* bestselling author

Today's world never stops—but for what? That's the challenge Alisha gives us in *Chasing Perfect*: What are you really chasing? Because we'll never find what we're looking for outside of Jesus. Culture remains steady to offer counterfeit pursuits, complete with false promises, but the truth remains: Only Jesus satisfies. If you're ready to have a cut-the-fluff convo about full-fledged surrender, this book is the real talk your soul craves.

—**Michelle Myers**, founder of she works HIS way

One of the things I love most about Alisha is her consistent, steadfast message of truth in the face of all the world is trying to feed us as Christian women today. She is on a mission to disassemble the lie that anything other than Jesus will satisfy our deepest longings and give us the peace we are so desperate for. This book was written for this time in the history of our nation and world. I couldn't be more excited about the message.

—**Cherice Stoltzfus**, founder and president of Nameless Collaborative

Resting in Christ amid the hustle culture—this Alisha Illian knows deep in her bones. *Chasing Perfect* is littered with authentic experience, biblical truth, and gospel application. Personal stories combined with Scripture narratives distill hope for the reader with both real depth and practical application. Alisha calls us to ferociously and faithfully pursue the person of Christ while humbly resting in his perfection rather than our own. May this book continue to be a balm of grace, curating a gospel hope in the midst of all of our daunting imperfections and overwhelming circumstances. While reading *Chasing Perfect*, you'll probably laugh, shed a tear or two, and, most importantly, be all the more compelled to chase perfect in knowing, loving, and beholding King Jesus.

—**Lacey Stevenson**, writer and Bible teacher | former minister at The Village Church, Dallas

As women, we know all too well the struggle of feeling that we have to be perfect. I know I do. In *Chasing Perfect*, Alisha speaks right to our hearts through relatable stories, reminding us that perfection is not the goal for our lives…a relationship with Christ is. If you find yourself struggling with the pressure of being perfect, pick up this book and be encouraged—you are not alone.

—**Angela Perritt**, founder and director of Love God Greatly

In a world filled with airbrushed illusions of flawless living and endless images of women somehow doing it all, Alisha uses *Chasing Perfect* to invite us to escape the quicksand of perfectionism. She shows us that the "more" we desire isn't found in doing more, going after more or even being more efficient, but instead in becoming relentlessly surrendered. A must read for every woman who is sick of striving and ready for a roadmap to trading perfectionism for presence and doing for divine purpose.

—**Marshawn Evans Daniels**, Godfidence Coach® | TV personality | reinvention strategist for women | founder of SheProfits.com

Chasing Perfect

ALISHA ILLIAN

HARVEST HOUSE PUBLISHERS
EUGENE, OREGON

Cover design by Kara Klontz Design

Cover photo © Mari Dein / Shutterstock

For bulk, special sales, or ministry purchases, please call 1-800-547-8979.
Email: Customerservice@hhpbooks.com

Chasing Perfect
Copyright © 2020 by Alisha Illian
Published by Harvest House Publishers
Eugene, Oregon 97408
www.harvesthousepublishers.com

ISBN 978-0-7369-8044-9 (pbk)
ISBN 978-0-7369-8045-6 (eBook)

Library of Congress Cataloging-in-Publication Data

Names: Illian, Alisha, author.
Title: Chasing perfect : peace and purpose in the exhausting pursuit o
    something better / Alisha Illian.
Description: Eugene, Oregon : Harvest House Publishers, 2020. | Summary:
    "Do you find yourself trying to make everything look good and you wind
    up missing the truly good moments? Alisha Illian wants you to know that
    you don't need perfect-you need perfect surrender to find freedom and
    peace"-- Provided by publisher.
Identifiers: LCCN 2020018198 (print) | LCCN 2020018199 (ebook) | ISBN
    9780736980449 (pbk) | ISBN 9780736980456 (ebook)
Subjects: LCSH: Women--Religious life. | Perfection--Religious
    aspects--Christianity. | Submissiveness--Religious
    aspects--Christianity.
Classification: LCC BV4527 .I375 2020 (print) | LCC BV4527 (ebook) | DDC
    248.8/43--dc23
LC record available at https://lccn.loc.gov/2020018198
LC ebook record available at https://lccn.loc.gov/2020018199

Printed in the United States of America

                20 21 22 23 24 25 26 27 28 / VP-SK / 10 9 8 7 6 5 4 3 2 1

You therefore must be perfect,
as your heavenly Father is perfect.

MATTHEW 5:48

For Jesus,
my perfection

CONTENTS

Introduction

was sitting in the Starbucks parking lot, sipping on a green tea latte, checking my text messages when my ten-year-old son, Reign, asked the question. "Mom, why are we here?"

A little surprised at his insightful question, I quickly shifted gears to try to make it a teachable moment.

But I first thought, *I think we're here to turn up the radio, roll down the windows, and sing at the top of our lungs, unconsciously botching the chorus with our own made-up lyrics.*

We're here to invite all the kids in the neighborhood to an epic game of Wiffle ball while the sprinklers turn us into wet noodles. As we twirl across the grass like newborn giraffes, we'll keep score by counting grass stains and giggles.

We're here to purposely show up late for basketball practice because we were digging for worms in the front yard with the priceless silver spoons passed down from Great-Great-Grandma Way-Too-Proper.

We're here to log off of Facebook, block Instagram, unpin from Pinterest, and take as many pictures and videos of the marshmallow-eating contest as possible, laughing uncontrollably while our siblings try to sing happy birthday with their cheeks full of white puffs. Our sore abs and cramped cheeks will say more than the best status update ever could.

We're here to have dinner with people whose skin color, hair style, music tastes, and tax bracket are nothing like ours. And more importantly, we're here to learn that their heartaches, dreams, passions, and hopes for their lives are exactly like ours.

When we are shuffling toward the grave, gumming our food and organizing our pills, I don't think we'll wish we spent more time in the office, going blind from account numbers and fluorescent lights. We'll be telling the nurses about that time when the cutest-little-thing-you-ever-did-see, covered in glitter and missing two front teeth, pranced joyfully on our leather loafers at her first daddy-daughter dance. We're here to notice that happiness just walked by wearing flippers and a cowboy hat and playing the kazoo.

As I snapped back to reality, I realized my inquisitive son was impatiently staring at me from the back seat.

"Buddy, we are here for so many reasons. But most importantly, we are here to love God more than anything and share His love with everyone we meet. Does that answer your question?"

After a short pause, Reign answered, "No, not really."

"What were you expecting?" I asked.

"I was just wondering what we are doing *here*," Reign said, pointing to the parking lot. "We were supposed to pick up Sage from volleyball practice 30 minutes ago."

Some of you may be asking the same question Reign was: What are we doing *here*? It's easy to get caught up in planning meals, hustling at work, satisfying your man, and taxiing kids around…and then feel exhausted at the end of the day. As women, we long for purpose. And peace. And direction. We are all chasing after the perfect little life, but underneath the glowing posts we share on social media, our faith feels stagnant and God seems distant.

If motherhood is kicking your rear, singleness is leaving you lonely, your job is monotonous, the expectations are endless, or your marriage is empty, this book is for you. If you feel grumpy, anxious, exhausted, irritable, and restless, my prayer is that the journey through these pages will spark a new hope for you.

God has a purpose for each of us, and the satisfaction we seek isn't found in retail therapy, self-help, and hustle. It's found in a person, Jesus Christ. And the secret you are about to learn is that perfection isn't found in chasing all the things, but in a relationship with the Savior of your soul.

So grab a warm beverage and your comfy slippers. We're going to learn how to start chasing Perfect.

1

Spent

You make known to me the path of life.

PSALM 16:11 NIV

You don't have time for this.

The laundry is piling up, grocery shopping needs to get done, and your lovable family dog just rolled in goose poop. And now he's sitting on your cream-colored suede couch. Next to your son's unfinished homework. You're supposed to call the babysitter to confirm Friday night, but you haven't really talked to your husband since that fight last week.

Or maybe you are rushing out the door for the umpteenth time, fighting back both the traffic and the tears. You never imagined you'd be a single parent in your mid-thirties, and your daily life is a continuous treadmill, where the speed and incline keep increasing. You don't know if your emotional legs can keep up.

Or perhaps you woke up with a heavy heart this morning. You thought a quality education and a great job would catapult you into a life of happiness, but you feel heavy and defeated. Even though you attend a great church with a thriving singles group, you are going through guys faster than you can swipe left and the dream of a family is fading. You'd stop and cry about it, but you don't have time to fix your makeup.

Something is seriously wrong, and it's not just the fact that you stayed in your pajama pants until noon.

It's the daily grind. It's the schedules we keep, the activities we commit to, and the plans we make. The plain old ordinary, mundane rhythm of activities keeps chipping away at our souls as we chase the perfect life.

As I was burning dinner the other night, I was listening to a show on the National Geographic channel. Two deep-sea diving experts were discussing the physics of a submarine. I found it fascinating that every square inch of a submarine's hull can withstand 580 pounds of pressure. The deeper the vessel submerges, the more pressure is exerted on the structure. As I sat there wondering how a submarine isn't completely destroyed by the extreme environment it must function in, it hit me:

What's on the inside has to be stronger than what's on the outside.

The same can be said about our lives. And our souls.

It's not the endless laundry to fold, bottoms to wipe, and toys to pick up. It's not the aging parents or wrinkling skin. It's not the sagging jeans or the muffin top. These are all external factors, and even if we learn how to prioritize better, find the best yes, or do the next right thing, we are still going to feel thousands of pounds of pressure every day. We have to strengthen what's on the inside if we want to deal with what's on the outside.

We feel spent because our souls are depleted. We are chasing after perfect in our relationships, jobs, and activities, but we are still discontent. Our souls are crying out for purpose and stability. Our world feels smaller than it should, and we feel a bit insignificant. The random pedicures and late-night drinks are not the panacea we were hoping for. At the end of the day, we've begun to realize that perhaps the perfect we've been searching for isn't in all the things.

Perhaps it's in a relationship.

> You can eat all the kale,
>
> buy all the things,
>
> lift all the weights,
>
> take all the trips,
>
> trash all that doesn't spark joy,
>
> wash your face and hustle like mad,
>
> but if you don't rest your soul in Jesus,
>
> you'll never find peace and purpose.

OUR LIVES AND SOULS

In Matthew 11:28-29, Jesus eloquently stated, "Come to me, all who labor and are heavy laden, and I will give you rest. Take my yoke upon you, and learn from me, for I am gentle and lowly in heart, and you will find rest for your souls." This verse is often quoted by well-meaning pastors in their sermons and on podcasts for good reason. Because we feel completely exhausted, teachers want to remind us that in Christ, we can find rest. Not any old get-a-good-night-sleep rest, but the deep, peaceful soul rest we've been seeking.

Jesus does offer us rest. But that's not all Jesus said. In fact, I probably read this verse a hundred times before I began to understand the message within the message. And I'm certain I'm still just scratching the surface.

In these verses Jesus is offering an open invitation for all of us who are labored and burdened, worn out and weary, sleep-deprived and depressed, to come to Him. He does not show any favoritism. With open arms, He gladly embraces all of us. He is directing us—perhaps even pleading with us—to come to Him for rest. Our Savior knows we will habitually go to shopping, social media, friends, or drinks instead of turning to Him. So He reminds us that true rest is found only in Him.

This isn't just good news; this is *the* news! The God of the universe is telling us that we should unload our worries on Him and He'll take care of them. We don't have to carry the burden of a cheating spouse, an empty womb, or an unfulfilling job with us. We can lay down our pain and pick up His peace.

But then He says something that blows my mind. He says, "After you put down *your* burdens, pick up *My* burdens and let's walk them out together. Then you will find peace for your souls." This is what He means by "take my yoke upon you and learn from me."

For us city folks, a yoke is a wooden crosspiece that fastens over the necks of two animals, typically oxen or horses, so that they can plow a field or pull a cart together. Farmers used to believe that if one ox could pull 500 pounds, then two oxen harnessed together could pull 1,000 pounds. But in reality, when two oxen are yoked, they can pull in excess of 1,250 pounds.

What Christ is sharing with us is transformational and counter-intuitive. He is saying that we are spent not because we are carrying things, but because we are carrying the *wrong* things. He is saying we are exhausted not because we are plowing the field, but because we are plowing the *wrong* fields. He is saying we are overwhelmed not because we are doing too much, but because we are doing too much on our own power.

Our souls are suffocating.

So we should probably stop and ask, what exactly is the soul and how do we keep it healthy?

The word *soul* is used many different ways. We've heard the soul must feel its worth. We are told it can be bought, sold, and lost. We've heard Jesus is the lover of our souls. In the Psalms, the soul sings, pants, and thirsts. We have soul survivors and listen to soul music. We pray the Lord our souls to keep. When we look into someone's eyes, we often say you can see into their soul.

All these phrases make the soul feel very magical and mysterious. But if we are to fully understand the emptiness keeping us up at night, we have to make the soul more tangible and real, with a respect for its eternal significance.

When struggling to grasp a complex concept we're often told, "If you can't explain it to a six-year-old, you don't understand it yourself." Since most six-year-olds have the attention span of an over-caffeinated gnat, I'll try to keep it simple:

You are like an iPhone.

The physical phone is your body, but the software—the operating system that makes everything work together—is your soul. Your soul integrates all aspects of who you are and what makes you unique.

> We are spent not because we are carrying things, but because we are carrying the *wrong* things.

All the aspects of your life—your mind, will, emotions, conscience, and heart—rely on your soul. Your soul is the operating software, and all the various roles you play are simply applications that live on top of it. The role of mom is an app that relies on the stability of the soul. The role of a loving spouse is an app that feeds on the health of the soul. If you find yourself melting down, struggling to communicate, or feeling depressed, it is not because the circumstances are unbearable. It is because there is something wrong with your soul. And when the operating system crashes, all the applications go dark.

The health of your soul is crucial to living a godly and productive life. With that in mind, we should pause and ask ourselves some poignant questions:

How many roles can I truly handle? In today's feminine-empowered world, we are told we can do and be anything. We can lead companies, families, and small European nations. We can glide into board meetings and family meetings sporting a cute pair of heels and balancing a briefcase and a diaper bag. While I'm certainly a proponent of using our God-given gifts, it's foolishness to act like Wonder Woman. We are beautifully and wonderfully made, but we have limits. When we redline our calendars and our hearts, we come to a breaking point.

How am I nourishing my soul? If you fail to upgrade the software on your phone, all the apps will begin to slow, freeze, and eventually crash. The same can be said of your soul. Throughout the book we'll talk about how we can feed our souls on a daily basis, but just know that "nourishing our souls" is different from "escaping." We are quite skilled at finding activities—whether it be purchasing purses or sipping lattes—that help us escape. But an escape is putting a Band-Aid on a gunshot wound. We are only distracting ourselves, not feeding our souls.

> If you find yourself melting down, struggling to communicate, or feeling depressed, it is not because the circumstances are unbearable. It is because there is something wrong with your soul.

Am I listening to my soul? This is so critical. All day long we are bombarded with people's needs: "What's for dinner?" "Can we have sex tonight?" "Your kid just puked in his kindergarten class." And we have to respond to each one of them. It's exhausting. But are we listening to the deeper cries that stem from our souls? They aren't as loud or as obvious as the ones that fill our minds and calendars. But they are the ones that will alert us to stress, anxiety, and depression. They are also the ones that will help us recharge and recover.

Of course, our iPhone won't work at all if it hasn't been charged. It has no power of its own. For the Christian, the power source is Jesus Christ. He is the sustainer and giver of life. Just like our phones must be charged regularly, our souls must charge daily. Hourly. Continuously. We are renewed and restored when we are plugged in to Jesus through prayer, time in the Word, and meaningful community with other believers.

Most of us are addicted to our iPhones. We rarely put them down and we monitor them constantly. If we are going somewhere, we check them for directions. If we want an update on the weather, we consult the touch screen. Whenever an aspect of our life needs guidance, we turn to the glowing box.

It's time we have this same maniacal, obsessed focus on the Life-giver of our souls.

COUNTING THE MOMENTS

I once gifted my husband a container of small stones on his birthday. I'm thoughtful like that. Each stone represented a month we had remaining until our children left home. While some may consider this a countdown to freedom, we have different intentions. We use the stones as reminders that even though the days seem long, the years are short. We have to live each exhausting moment of parenthood with intentionality and purpose, joyfully celebrating the gift of time and the brevity of life.

I've been blessed with three wonderful kids. They are constantly testing my patience and the hardwood floors, but I can't imagine life without them. Reign is twelve, and the prototypical firstborn. He's an introvert and a perfectionist who can typically be found with either a football or basketball in his hands. The only thing bigger than his desire to win is his heart for Jesus, and I almost tear up every time he says a prayer.

Sage is ten and has already claimed the title jack-of-all-trades. She likes volleyball, basketball, swimming, piano, art, theater, school, Bible study, and about a dozen other activities that all practice on Monday. She is always smiling and joyful. I'm a bit biased, but I think she attacks life like Tarzan and is as beautiful as Jane.

And then there is Rogue. He is eight and lives up to his name. He is the youngest, and he is incredibly smart and fun. Everyone at school, regardless of their grade, knows Rogue. To him, no one is a stranger and everyone is a target, either for a high five or a forearm shiver. He's got the Brad Pitt charm going on, but I don't fall for it. Too often, at least. When he asked to be baptized last summer at Pine Cove Christian camp and then clearly articulated his need for grace, I melted. He does that to me.

As I was watching the three of them play a game the other day that would most likely end up in an ER visit, God granted me one of those rare moments of clarity. I realized I only have a dozen more summers until all three of them leave the house. After that, there will be no more ice cream truck stops, pool floaties to blow up, or neighborhood Nerf gun wars to monitor. I only have about 20 family trips left. We always make such great memories snow skiing, zip-lining, and swimming, but we rarely get to take more than a couple excursions a year. I've always thought we'd have an endless number of SUV road trips, but I can now count them on my hands and feet.

When my kids were little, they always shouted, "Love you to heaven and back!" and "Love you more than you love me!" when they went to bed. But they aren't little anymore. I can't count how many times I'll hear these good-night phrases in years anymore; it may just be months.

We like pizza at our house and probably eat it once a week. Don't judge. I make salmon from time to time too. If I'm doing my math correctly, we have around 416 more pizzas to eat together. This number may push out my waistline, but it pulls on my soul.

If we pray with them every day, we only have 4,380 more prayers left. Granted, our spiritual modeling and encouragement will continue into their adulthood, but not in the same way. We will continue to pray for our children, but not likely sitting bedside as we tenderly tuck them in snug as a bug in a rug. We constantly preach that relying on God is the most important thing, but the number of times we can exemplify this while they are under our roof is limited.

It may be hard to believe, but my kids argue. And fight. And occasionally say mean things to one another. Whether it is about Fortnite or who sits in the front seat of the car, they can be selfish little minions, which doesn't surprise me since we are related. But I only have a few hundred more opportunities to teach them about conflict resolution and model for them the grace of the gospel. These teachable moments will have to guide them in future conversations with their boss and spouse and their own children.

If I subtract the sleeping hours, I only have 61,320 more hours until Rogue leaves the house. I have even less with Reign and Sage. Somehow I have to squeeze in time to teach them how to make their bed, hit a jump shot, read their Bible, control their hormones, rejoice in suffering, navigate the Internet, live in thankfulness, drive the car, and give grace to others.

The rocks are slipping away fast. Sure, I will still be their mom, and God willing, I will still have opportunities to teach them as they grow, but those moments will be different. Embracing these opportunities now fills my soul. But I also wrestle with God and my feelings of anxiousness, nervousness, and inadequacy.

Fortunately, I'm not the first person to wrestle with God. Jacob wrestled with God all night. Maybe you understand a little of what he felt. Jacob, whose name meant "deceiver" or literally "grabber," had known a life of constant struggle and fear. He had served Laban, his father-in-law, for 20 years. Worried that Laban would not let him depart, he secretly fled with all that he had. He was about to encounter his older brother, Esau, who was embittered over a stolen birthright. Because he feared for his life, Jacob hoped to keep his brother from harming him by sending gifts, women, and children along the River Jabbok.

So there Jacob was, surrounded by his enemies, stripped of his possessions, helpless, and out of control. He was out of tactics. He was out of strategies.

He was exactly where God wanted him.

Jacob was in a place of complete dependence, and God needed to do a work in Jacob's heart. He needed Jacob to see that nothing could be accomplished apart from Him. Jacob was missing the only thing that mattered.

After a long night of struggle, God did bless Jacob. He changed his name and identity from Jacob to Israel, which means "one who wrestles with God." But the blessing came with pain. God tweaked Jacob's hip permanently. No more CrossFit for Jacob. He needed a reminder that his ultimate purpose and peace would not be found in his abilities, but in God.

> Don't miss the blessing buried in the busy.

Although our daily struggles manifest themselves in different ways, they are like Jacob's limp. They are reminders of the good stuff. The endless pile of laundry reminds us that we are blessed to have a family. The minefield of Legos reminds us that we have kids who love to play. The pile of bills reminds us that we have indoor bathrooms and a roof over our heads.

We spend ourselves in all sorts of various ways, but don't miss the blessing buried in the busy. Our limps remind us that we desperately need God and that He's always with us. God's deliverance is His presence. Remember to count the moments. It's the good stuff.

RAGING PEACE

You probably don't know Gracia Burnham, but you should. In my opinion, she is one of the rare few who have discovered the secret to finding peace and purpose.

Gracia has three children, two boys and a girl. For 17 years, she and her husband, Martin, served with New Tribes Mission in the Philippines. Martin was a jungle pilot, and his job consisted of delivering mail, supplies, and encouraging messages and transporting the sick and injured to various medical facilities. Gracia supported him while homeschooling their children.

Everything changed on May 27, 2001, on their eighteenth wedding anniversary. During their celebration, the Burnhams were taken captive by a militant group of Muslims called the Abu Sayyaf Group. Along with other guests, they were taken to an ASG stronghold on Basilan Island.

Over the course of the next year they were constantly moved to new locations, living in primitive jungle conditions, evading Philippine military capture, withstanding gun battles, and experiencing unimaginable atrocities. Some of the hostages were killed and others were released, but the Burnhams remained in captivity.

After the events of September 11, 2001, the news media took great interest in the Burnham story and made it a national headline. The Philippine military felt the pressure and attempted a rescue mission. Tragically, Martin was killed by gunfire during the conflict. Gracia was wounded but rescued and returned home safely.[1] She now resides just minutes from where I live in Kansas. She has authored two books and spends her time testifying to God's goodness and the many lessons she had learned during her captivity. When asked about her life, she responds, "The Lord's mercies are new every morning. Great is His faithfulness."

Most women feel as though they give, give, give all day long. We give to ministries, the neighbors, our jobs, and the local PTA. We fill the roles of taxi driver, chef, teacher, and lover. We run to the grocery store and through the carpool line when all we really want to run is a bubble bath. We feel called to give sacrificially of ourselves, but it is wearing us out. How do faithful women like Gracia stoke the internal fire to continuously serve? More importantly, how do they find peace amid such suffering and chaos? I think we often confuse peace with ease. Ease is comfort and convenience. Peace is a deep, settled soul unwavered by circumstance. Jesus never promised a life of ease, but He did say we would have supernatural peace when we trust Him.

For a long time I've wrestled over this idea, thinking that to really allow my soul to regain strength I'd need to get radical. I'd need to cut off the hand that causes the brokenness, to rid the sin that entangles me. Burn the kids' sport schedules! Toss the phone out the window! Quit all church activities! No more of anything. It's all or nothing. I struggle tremendously with navigating the middle ground, and my soul grows weary in the tension.

It's not reasonable to believe that all the activities are going to stop or that we can just bail on them. We can't. We are breadwinners and homemakers and lovers and nurturers and more. But we can reorient our lives so that we are focusing on the things that bring real peace and purpose. Instead of chasing after all the supposedly perfect things in the world, we can start by chasing after the real Perfect—our Savior, Jesus Christ. And then all our efforts can flow from there.

God knows a woman's heart. He knows we are anxious about every-thing. He knows we need a raging peace—a peace so overwhelming and powerful that it surpasses all understanding as it guards our hearts and minds.

THE SECRET

Lots of stories in the Bible can resonate with our hearts as women. But the one that I think unpacks the mystery of chasing Perfect is Jesus' conversation with Mary and Martha.

In Luke 10:38, we find Jesus entering the village of Bethany. Martha, her sister, Mary, and her brother, Lazarus, lived there and welcomed Jesus and His followers into their home. In the passage, Mary was sitting at the feet of Jesus, listening to His teaching.

Martha, on the other hand, was fulfilling the job description of a typical woman of that time. She was in the kitchen serving. As Martha was running around handling all the preparations, she became angry with her idle sister. Finally, she had enough and marched right over to Jesus and told Him, "Make Mary help me."

At that moment I can only imagine Jesus cracked a small and compassionate smile. He sensed her anger and distraction. He felt her worry and anxiety. He knew—just as He knows with each one of us right now—that she needed a mighty word of truth that would call her to a greater purpose and deeper peace. So He gently replied, "Martha, Martha, you are worried and bothered about so many things; but *only one thing* is necessary" (verses 41-42, emphasis added).

This book is about that one thing. And that one thing changes everything.

2

Only One Thing

One thing is necessary. Mary has chosen the good
portion, which will not be taken away from her.

LUKE 10:42

When God doesn't have your attention, He will disturb what does. While this may be inconvenient, it is actually a great mercy, because anything apart from Him will ultimately leave us empty and flailing.

Jesus stopped Martha in her tracks when He said her name. When I was a kid, I knew some profound correction was coming if Mom said my name more than once. It was her way of getting my immediate attention. Jesus did the same with Martha. He said her name not once, but twice. Directly and gently, He called her by name and then admonished her behavior with great compassion. With a few intentional words, He helped Martha realize He didn't have her full attention.

And if something doesn't have your full attention, it doesn't have your full affection.

God doesn't take a back seat. He isn't plan B. As the Creator of

> Our priorities reflect what we worship.

the universe, He deserves to be first and foremost in our lives. Martha was learning that even though she was doing all sorts of good things, she had her priorities backward. We often talk about priorities as if they can be quickly corrected and their order is not of all that much importance. In reality, they are a reflection of our hearts and what we deem to be important. Our priorities reflect what we worship.

Jesus wasn't just trying to get Martha's attention and affection—He was trying to get to her heart.

THE PROBLEM WITH MARTHA

It's easy to give Martha a hard time, but just look at the situation. Not only did the long-awaited Messiah show up at her front door unannounced, but according to Luke 10:17, He brought 72 of His closest friends with Him. No text message. No warning. No call-ahead seating. Jesus just showed up and had a whole ragamuffin band with Him.

At my house, this would warrant a full-out, five-alarm fire drill. When Jason has the audacity to even invite a colleague over for coffee, I panic. I feel the need to vacuum the house, wash the dog, scrub the counters, and order a new set of coffee mugs from Amazon. And this is for a person we already know. So I understand why Martha was a bit overwhelmed about the unannounced entourage.

Yet despite the tough circumstances, Martha still had the courage to "welcome them" to her home. Surely we can give Martha a little grace, right?

What happened after Jesus and the disciples entered her home, however, is the most telling part. She immediately got busy. She started working the kitchen, preparing the pita, arranging the table, and attending to everyone's comfort in efforts to be the perfect host. I can only imagine the stress of trying to find a hummus recipe on Pinterest that feeds that many people and takes five minutes or less to make! I'm certain that in her own mind, Martha thought she was doing a charitable act of service. Being hospitable and serving others is, after all, biblical. Jesus Himself stated,

> Who then is the faithful and wise servant, whom his master has set over his household, to give them their food at the proper time? Blessed is that servant whom his master will find so doing when he comes (Matthew 24:45-46).

So Jesus' correction doesn't seem to make sense. Only when we take a closer look at the text and study Jesus exact words does God start to reveal the true message. Jesus wasn't condemning Martha's service or hospitality. He was concerned that Martha was distracted and that she was trying to do *more than was necessary*. He was concerned about her heart.

The Greek word for distraction is *perispao*, which means "to be drawn away, over-occupied, too busy and driven away mentally about a thing." And the Greek word for anxious is *merimna*, which means, "to seek to promote one's own interest."

Too busy. Over-occupied. Self-interested. Any of these things ring true in your own life?

The only necessary thing was to spend time with the Savior. But instead of finding emotional and spiritual rest with Jesus, Martha was troubling herself with all the preparations surrounding Him. And because Jesus looks at the heart and not our outward actions, He realized Martha was preoccupied and stressed.

Too often, we value situations based on *what* was done and not *why* it was done. Jesus is always looking for the why. Feeding the hungry, sheltering the homeless, and caring for widows are all excellent acts of service. But if you are performing them so that you get the glory or so that others applaud your kindness, you have failed on the *why*. Christ desires for us to perform these kind acts, but not because they draw likes on Facebook or accolades from church members. He wants us to do so because they point people to Jesus, the ultimate *why*.

Like so many of us, Martha was succeeding on the *what*, but she was failing on the *why*. Her service was driven from an inner desire to promote her own interests through her own strength. She was serving with the wrong motive. She was likely overwhelmed because she was trying to prove her value and worth by how she performed. She was overwhelmed by her agenda rather than by Jesus.

And Martha wasn't just looking at her agenda, but at her sister. Mary was *sitting* at the feet of Jesus. How infuriating! Too often I'm like Martha and I'll look outward, around, through, and over at a situation. I look everywhere but up. Everywhere but toward the Savior.

The crazy thing is that Martha forgot *whom* she was talking to. She was addressing the Lord of the universe, Creator God, the Alpha and the Omega. The *why* was right in front of her, smiling compassionately and loving on her troubled heart. Martha wanted Jesus to fix the situation with Mary; Jesus wanted to fix Martha.

Martha missed it. And we often miss it too. We think we have to handle everything on our own. We feel responsible. We see what isn't fair and complain. We don't ask God; we tell Him. We forget the power of His presence. And we doubt that He cares for our needs even though He is sitting right in front of us. When we take our focus off the Lord, we start pursuing joy and satisfaction in the number on the scale, the trip we have planned next summer, our husband's affection level, the date we have scheduled over the weekend, our children's report card, or a clean bill of health. When our joy is dependent on other things, we can fall into despair, anxiety, and depression.

Productivity is not merely the measure of what got done, but of who was loved. Martha desperately wanted to do the right thing, but she got distracted. She let her actions override her affections and tried to do more than was necessary. And that's something I can relate to. And maybe you can too.

THE PROMISE OF MARY

Now let's talk about sweet little Mary. While her sister was running around the house, trying to take care of their guests, Mary was just sitting and listening to Jesus. And she was commended for it. In fact, she was not only commended, but Jesus was so bold as to say, "Only one thing is needed. Mary has chosen the good portion, which will not be taken away from her."

While it doesn't seem like a big deal to the twenty-first-century reader that Mary was sitting at the feet of Jesus, it was actually a very bold and courageous move. To sit at the feet of a rabbi and listen to his teaching was an indication of a desire to become a rabbi in the future. Only men were afforded this privilege, but Mary didn't hesitate to break the cultural norm and snuggle up to the Savior.

> If you are performing so that you get the glory or so that others applaud your kindness, you have failed on the *why*.

She was always doing things a little unconventionally—sitting at the feet of the Rabbi, anointing His feet with expensive perfume and wiping it off with her hair (John 12:1-3), and moving Jesus to tears when her brother, Lazarus, had died (John 11:32-33). Mary didn't let her culture's gender roles dictate her actions. She knew her worth resided in Jesus.

But was her heart completely pure in all of this? How could she not have noticed her sister's panic and stress? If nearly that many people showed up at my house unannounced, I'd need a catering service to make it through the evening. Shouldn't Mary have at least offered to help Martha with the appetizers, the napkins, or something?

At first blush, it appears Mary was taking the easy way out. She just plopped herself down on a throw pillow in front of Jesus and started taking notes. This doesn't seem like something that should have been encouraged. But Jesus said she had chosen the better portion.

Life is full of decisions. Sometimes we have to choose between good and evil, but in most daily circumstances we have to choose between good, better, and best. I think Jesus was referring to the latter in this conversation with Martha and Mary. He wasn't suggesting Martha's service to others was bad. In fact, it was a good thing. He was just reminding them that Mary's decision to sit with Jesus was better.

This may be an unpopular opinion, but resting in a hammock is not more spiritual or holy than hard work and service. That is not the point of this story. The best portion was not the simple act of rest from the busy of life, but rather the state of Mary's heart. She wasn't stressed, overwhelmed, or hurried inside. She wasn't trying to prove anything. Jesus wasn't concerned with Martha's activity level; He was concerned with her anxiety level. Martha could have chosen the better portion while she was still serving.

In contrast to her sister's busyness, Mary laid everything down in pursuit of Christ:

- Her pride—she was sitting at Jesus' feet.

- The approval of others—she didn't care what others thought of her actions.

- Her efforts to perform—she didn't need applause or accolades for a well-cooked meal.

- Her need to provide—she realized Jesus was the great Sustainer and Provider.

If Jesus wanted to multiply the hummus and pita, He could do it. If He wanted to turn water to wine, He was able. Mary realized Jesus was the ultimate Source of everything her heart desired and needed. She sensed it. She felt it. She believed it. Purpose was found in Him—not in her service, not in the approval of man, not in appearances, not in physical sustenance or a put-together home. In Him alone.

This story is a near perfect representation of our daily lives. The unexpected happens, our normal routine is thrown off, a number of rowdy and unpredictable people invade our lives, multiple activities beg for our attention, and yet those who are walking in faith still settle at the feet of Jesus. I long to be one of those faithful few.

I can't pretend to know what you are going through right now. Some of you may be struggling with an unfaithful or disconnected husband. Some of you may be overwhelmed by your job. Some of you may be exhausted by the never-ending list of kids' activities.

> Jesus wasn't concerned with Martha's activity level; He was concerned with her anxiety level.

Some of you may be broke, lonely, addicted, sick, depressed, anxious, or just frustrated with day-to-day life. Wherever you are and whatever you're going through, be like Mary—focused on nothing but God. In the storm of life, she sat and worshipped the Creator, not the created things. She wasn't focused on herself, her home, or the company. She focused on *only one thing*.

Jesus.

EMOTIONS AND TRUTH

In May 2019, Dave Gass, the former lead pastor at Grace Daily Fellowship and church planter at Journey the Way, decided to renounce his faith on social media. After 20 years of being an evangelical pastor, he wrote,

> My marriage was a sham, prayer was never answered, miracles were never performed. People died, children rebelled, marriages failed, addictions occurred—all at the same rate as nonbelievers. The system just doesn't work.[1]

My heart goes out to Dave. We need to pray for him.

But I find Dave's comments interesting. He referred to our walk with Christ as a "system" and not a relationship. He listed all the things in his life that didn't go as he had hoped, as if God were some divine vending machine that dispenses good things when you press the right buttons. It's as if he never read the Bible at all.

The people God loved went through all kinds of heartaches and troubles. When leaving Egypt, the Israelites marched through the desert for 40 years, even though the walk should have taken 14 days. Ten of the 12 original disciples were martyred—sawed in half, burned at the stake, crucified upside down. The only one who wasn't, died stranded on an island. God's only Son was tortured, beaten, and crucified naked on a Roman cross with the worst possible public humiliation. What part of any of this makes a believer think following Christ is smooth sailing? Jesus never said the Christian life would be easy or comfortable, but He did say it would be worth it.

Like many of us, Dave built his faith on experience and emotion. But God calls us to build ours on truth.

I'm a bottom-line kind of girl. I don't want all of the fluff—just tell me what I need to know. And fortunately, God is a bottom-line kind of God. All the stories, miracles, and journeys in the Bible point to one person—Jesus. And God makes it perfectly clear in His Word that our purpose in this life is to pursue and love Him completely, continuously, and fully. That's it. All the other things like obedience, sacrifice, fruit-bearing, discipling, our specific calling, and mission will be an outflow of this one necessary thing.

Does the simplicity surprise you? I'm guessing it might. We often overcomplicate faith. The hectic nature of everyday life overwhelms us. There are always clean clothes that need to be put away, whiny children who need a snack, and friends who are on the brink of divorce, a mental breakdown, or overdosing on chocolate. The demands on our waking hours naturally drive us to quick fixes and a list of solutions. But when we try to muster up the strength to tackle everything by our own, we miss the Lord's wisdom, which helps us identify our purpose and true calling.

As women, we are easily driven by experience and emotion. I'm no exception. When it comes to birthdays and other special days, I like to go big. Why just make a birthday cake when you could fill up the living room with 953 balloons, dress up the dogs with sombreros, and rent a mariachi band for the day? My wonderful husband, however, wasn't gifted the same celebratory spirit from the Lord. If joyful celebration were a 100-meter dash, he'd be the one showing up at the starting line wearing flippers and a snorkel.

So when Mother's Day came this year, I was secretly hoping for breakfast in bed, a video with all my best mom moments, an interpretive dance performed by all three kids, and a 17-page handmade card. But when I woke up, there was nothing. Nada. Zero. My kids didn't even say happy Mother's Day. And forget breakfast in bed. I had to get my own coffee.

As you can imagine, I was fuming. It didn't help that every other woman I knew was posting wonderful pictures on Facebook and Instagram of their thoughtful family. And I was stuck with these selfish Neanderthals.

Fortunately, God met me in my pity party in the middle of the day. Instead of focusing on this one experience and my expectations around it, He reminded me of the bigger truth: Jason loves me and consistently provides for me emotionally and spiritually 365 days a year. All my kids have a personal relationship with Jesus, and we have a roof over our head and shoes on our feet. He reminded me of the truth, not just my feelings.

Todd Wagner, the senior pastor at Watermark Church in Dallas, said, "Feelings are real, but they are not reliable."[2] But we are often driven by our emotions and feelings, which is why life can seem so overwhelming and confusing. On a high emotion day, we can have trouble picking out which jeans to wear, much less understanding our specific assignments as followers of Christ. We are tossed about, anchored to nothing, so we miss out on the big and exciting mission to further the kingdom, evangelize the world, disciple the nations, and use our spirit-given gifts to bless our families.

When Martha was upset that Mary wasn't helping her, she was relying on her experience and emotions. She missed the truth: the fact that the Savior was reclining next to her.

If you are a woman in America today, the culture is screaming at you. The feminist movement is demanding you dream big, hustle hard, and shoot for the top. Books are encouraging you to stop apologizing. Social media is telling you that you can accomplish whatever you want.

These messages are appealing. They speak to our flesh. They speak to our appetites. But they confuse our souls. They fail to point us back to the truth about our lives and our dreams, because they fail to point us back to God.

Your soul thirsts for the invisible, the eternal, and the meaningful. In 2 Corinthians 4:18, Paul reminds us to "fix our eyes not on what is seen, but on what is unseen, since what is seen is temporary, but what is unseen is eternal" (NIV). God knows if we focus our lives on what is visibly in front of us—whatever it is, either good or bad—it will take

His rightful place. And we'll become enslaved and exhausted from such things.

But here's the mystery of Christ that most people miss: our good comes when He gets the greatest glory. When we desire Him, delight in Him, pursue Him, and fill our hearts with Him, He gets the glory and we receive the very best of what He has for us.

When God becomes your everything, you can go through anything.

While this is certainly good news, some of you may have misread the sentence. I didn't say you could *be* anything. I didn't say you could *have* anything. I didn't say you could *do* anything. I said you could *go through* anything. In the journey of life, we all have to go through trials. The only question is whether you are going to face them alone or walk hand in hand with the Savior.

In the Old Testament, Job knew about trials. Job worshipped God and loved Him more than anything. But that didn't make him immune to troubles. Satan believed Job loved God simply because of the blessings—the land, resources, family, and health—that God gave him. Satan said Job would turn away from God as soon as the blessings were taken away.

But God knew Job's heart. He knew Job found his identity and satisfaction in Him. So He allowed Satan to strip Job of everything but his life. God even went so far as to allow painful boils, questionable friends, and an unimaginably grieved wife to plague the faithful man. In his humanity and flesh, Job suffered greatly. But even though his body shook, his soul remained calm.

Job lost everything, but he didn't lose hope. Because his hope was found in God.

We live in the constant demands of everyday life. We live with unreasonable job expectations, unpaid bills, urgent emails, and whiny toddlers. We live with the fear of coronavirus and spilled chocolate milk that is molding between the car seats. We live with the exhaustion of trying to find a single man who actually loves God and won't drop us the minute there are other options. We live with a cancer diagnosis and a child who is fighting ADHD and the bully at school. We live with unexpected late fees, another negative pregnancy test, and a body that resembles a pear more than an hourglass.

But with God, we will pass through these things. In Isaiah 43, the prophet states,

> When you pass through the waters,
>   I will be with you;
> and when you pass through the rivers,
>   they will not sweep over you.
> When you walk through the fire,
>   you will not be burned;
>   the flames will not set you ablaze.
> For I am the LORD your God (verses 2-3 NIV).

In the storms of life, you are not protected because of your umbrella of wisdom or exceptional planning skills. And you are not dodging the fire because of your flame-retardant bank account. You go through the trials unscathed for one reason only: because God is with you.

Dave Gass missed this. He was relying on the experience and emotions of his marriage, troubled kids, and unredeemed addictions. Even though he had served in the ministry for over 20 years, he believed only as far as his physical eyes could see. He missed the goodness and truth Job experienced from going through the storm with his focus on the eternal.

Jesus may roll off your lips or His name may be on the bumper sticker attached to your car, but unless He fills that sacred space in your heart and sits on the throne of your life, you will not experience peace. Because when God becomes your everything, you can go through anything.

ON MISSION

When I was young both in years and in my faith, I thought God wanted me to move to Africa. I even dreamed about living in a grass hut and walking around barefoot. I thought leaving America and becoming a missionary in a poor country was the ultimate act of obedience.

I was partially right. We *are* called to be on mission. We are called to sacrifice, take up our cross, and follow Christ as we make disciples of the nations. But it doesn't have to be in another nation, four plane flights away. We can, and should, be on mission right where we are.

If you are a stay-at-home mom, then your home is your mission field. If you have a full-time job, then the office is your mission field. When you are volunteering at a homeless shelter, working out at the gym, or eating at your favorite restaurant, you are in your mission field.

So if we are in our mission field, why are we not serving? I'd argue it's because we are too comfortable.

Paul shared some deep insights with the Philippian church that the Holy Spirit revealed to him, ones we need to hear today as well. He wrote that they would need to be "content in any and every situation, whether well fed or hungry, whether living in plenty or in want" (Philippians 4:12 NIV).

Why in the world would we need to be content in abundance?

Because we get comfortable in abundance and we lose sight of God. We focus on the created things, rather than on the Creator.

God made creation. He delights in His creation. He made humans to delight in His creation as well. That's why people have taste buds and nerve endings and pleasure receptors to experience and enjoy all the things He designed.

In His creative majesty, He equipped us to take pleasure in a lover's kiss, an arrangement of music, a basketball game, pepperoni pizza, and *Downton Abbey*. He lets us experience a beautiful beach, a joyful dog greeting us at the door, the wonderful aroma of a marinated steak, and a new shirt that fits just right. As image bearers of God, we were made to delight as He delights. The gifts we enjoy were meant to be enjoyed.

As long as they are in their rightful place.

This is the key to enjoying God's blessings. They have to remain in their rightful place. A car driving on the sidewalk or a fire burning in the middle of the living room can both cause massive destruction—not because there is anything wrong with a car or fire, but because these gifts were taken out of their element.

We have done the same with our stuff and blessings. And it's the primary reason most women feel lost, unsatisfied, and distant from God. It's the reason we are no longer on mission.

This was the case for the rich young ruler in Matthew 19. He had obeyed all the laws, attended church on Sunday, posted some random inspirational quotes on Twitter, but when Jesus asked him to sell all his possessions and follow Him, he caved. He then walked away from Jesus.

We are the rich young rulers. We worship comfort and abundance. The rich young ruler didn't want to let go of his possessions because he believed his joy and peace depended on them. But Jesus *is* joy and peace. None of the tangible, visible, or experiential blessings the Lord provides could ever fulfill like the Lord Himself. Christ was trying to help the young man see that if he removed the material distractions, he could see God as more precious, valuable, and life-giving than anything else.

It's true that throughout the Bible, God blessed many of His people with material blessings—Adam, Abraham, David, Solomon, Job, Lydia, Joseph of Arimathea, and even Mary, Martha, and Lazarus. All were known to have wealth and prosperity. But the material blessings and creature comforts were to be a reflection of the goodness of God, not a replacement for Him. God's people are always called to keep the Lord first and serve no other gods. When the divine order is reversed, we forget to be on mission right where we are.

**The problem isn't having all the things—
the problem is when all the things have us.**

I thought God wanted me to go to Africa so that I could serve Him with faithfulness and obedience. Turns out I had been standing in a fertile mission field all along, and all I had to do was start watering at my own feet.

The reason I didn't realize it then—and often don't realize it now—is because I'm distracted and enamored with my own comfort. And you are too. In the next few chapters, we are going to explore what it means to truly worship God and keep Him at the center of our lives. If you are feeling exhausted and spent, just hold on. The secret to being content starts right where you are and inside of you. And God is doing a good work to plant you firmly on solid ground.

We need to start with the Bible. Not with our feelings, our experiences, or our desires. Not with social media, the news, or tradition. Not even with religion or other believers. We need to start with the infallible Word of God and allow it to inform our hearts and direction.

Mary knew Jesus was the Word incarnate, which was why amid the hustle and bustle of the uninvited guests, she sat at His feet. Only when we spend time saturating and informing our minds with His Word, when we submit to the Spirit in prayer, and when we realign and renew our thinking around Jesus Christ will we start experiencing peace and purpose. God longs to create in us a new heart, but it starts with new affections, desires, and habits.

If you are going to deal with the hooligans in your home and the hustlers in the office, you're going to need more than empty prayers and positive vibes from the universe. You're going to need a personal, vibrant relationship with Christ and an accurate interpretation of His Word. God will do miraculous work *around* you after He has done miraculous work *within* you.

Martha didn't see this at first, but Mary did, which is why her problems became small, her worries insignificant, and her delight overwhelming. Mary's heart was overcome with the magnificent presence of the all-satisfying words of Jesus because she loved God more.

And that is the only thing that matters.

3

Inside Out

God is spirit and those who worship
him must worship in spirit.

JOHN 4:24

t was hot and dry in the deserts of Judea. Jesus and His disciples were
taking the exhausting journey toward Galilee. Surprisingly, He chose
the route that would take them through Samaria. This was a shocking
move because devout Jews always took the longer, more treacherous
route to the east and across the Jordan to avoid defilement by coming
into contact with the Samaritan people.

The Samaritans' ancestry was a mix of both Jew and Gentile (non-
Jew). They had their own version of the Pentateuch (first five books of
the Bible) and their own temple in which they worshipped on Mount
Gerizim. True Jews always shunned and avoided mingling with the
Samaritans. But not Jesus. In fact, He had a divine appointment with
one of them.

It was noon, the hottest part of the day, when Jesus came to the
town of Sychar, near the well of Jacob. Traveling at this time and
across these lands was not comfortable. There were no 7-Elevens or

convenience stores to fill a hungry belly or quench the desert thirst. If travelers were thirsty, they had to find a well.

Jesus was weary from His travel and sat down to rest while the disciples went into town to buy some food. After the disciples had walked away, a Samaritan woman came to the well to draw water. This was odd because women would never journey to the well in midday heat. Jesus would reveal later in their conversation that she was living in an immoral situation, and her behavior would have been considered utterly despicable.

So perhaps she was coming in the middle of the day to avoid the other women. Maybe she wanted to hide her shame. Or she could have been bullied, shunned, and made to feel like an outcast. Regardless of the exact reason, she was operating out of the norm and was most likely quite lonely.

But Jesus spoke to her.

This was astonishing. A Jewish man was not only speaking to a Samaritan, He was speaking to an immoral, female Samaritan. And out in the open for everyone to see! I thought I was breaking cultural norms by allowing my boys to wear shorts in December, but I'm an amateur.

Jesus is an expert. Even as He rests by the well, He shows us the way to reach out to the lost. We don't need some 12-step evangelical strategy or preplanned outreach event to reach those who need Jesus. We just have to be willing to engage in day-to-day situations. We can initiate meaningful conversations at the campus cafeteria, the local beauty salon, or over a Chick-fil-A sandwich while the kids are sharing germs in the play area. We can infuse God-conversation into anything and everything we do. This is what Jesus did, and He did it with a woman no one else would dare approach. He was preparing not only to change her heart but to also redefine what it means to *worship*.

Jesus began the conversation when He asked her for a drink. Understandably, she was taken aback. She immediately questioned why He was speaking to her, given the precarious situation.

Jesus replied, "If you knew the gift of God, and who it is that is saying to you, 'Give me a drink,' you would have asked him, and he would have given you living water" (John 4:10).

The Samaritan woman was confused. She didn't know what Jesus was trying to say. So she responded by reminding Him that He had nothing with which to draw out the water.

But Jesus was not talking about physical water. He was not talking about the wetness that quenches the thirst of the body, but the spiritual water that saturates and quenches the deepest droughts of the soul.

He was talking about Himself.

Still confused, she proceeded to ask Him a bit snarkily where this special well was located.

Jesus knew what was going on. The Samaritan woman was bound up by tradition and cultural norms, seeing only what was right in front of her eyes. She couldn't see with spiritual eyes—at least not yet. So with compassion and great patience, Jesus told her that if she were to drink from His well, she would never thirst again. His water would become in her a spring of water welling up to eternal life.

Intrigued, the woman finally asked Jesus to give her this miraculous water. And He did. But not in the way she expected.

He asked her to call on her husband. This was obviously a sensitive subject. Jesus knew this, but He wasn't afraid to go to the hard place. He knew the Samaritan woman had to admit to the truth, which was ugly and shameful, before she could really desire the living water or embrace grace.

I wonder how many times we are reluctant to have hard conversations. We don't want to offend someone or step on their toes. We don't want to experience an awkward moment or have a difficult conversation. But a person's eternal life is on the line. And as Jesus demonstrated, it's often necessary to speak truth, which includes conversations about promiscuity, addiction, and pride. When we waltz around hard conversations, we water down the gospel. But when we engage people on hard but truthful topics, we allow the living water to flow. And it goes straight to the heart.

The Samaritan women felt the weight of Jesus' words. But she was accustomed to skirting around truth, so she replied, "I have no husband" (verse 17). While this was technically accurate, Jesus revealed the real truth: she had been disgracefully divorced five times and was currently living with a man who was not her husband. The man she was living with was quite possibly the only man who would take her in.

The Samaritan woman felt exposed. This strange but kind Jewish man spoke openly about her shameful past when others would not even look her way. She wasn't sure what to do. I'm not sure how I would have reacted. I get creeped out when I search for a new vacuum on Google and within a minute start getting ads about Dysons and Hoovers on my social media feed.

Her knee-jerk reaction was to turn the conversation toward religion. It may have been a bait-and-switch move, a way of trying to distract from the sensitive personal subject Jesus had hit on, but our Lord was not phased. He used the detour to shed some groundbreaking insight on what it means to worship.

> When we engage people on hard but truthful topics, we allow the living water to flow.

The Samaritan woman told Jesus that her forefathers believed the proper place of worship should be on Mount Gerizim, but for a Jew, worship happened in Jerusalem. Her understanding of religion involved *something to do* and a *specific place in which to do it*.

This was where Jesus dropped the mic. Jesus told her the time had now come when worship would not be held on a mountain, in Jerusalem, or at a local church, but that true worshippers will worship the Father "in spirit and truth" (verse 23). Jesus was saying it wasn't about something to do or a place in which to do it. It was about aligning one's heart with God and living intimately with Him.

This was radical talk. This was "stop associating with your local denomination" talk. This was "rip the Jesus fish off your car" talk. This was "stop calling yourself a conservative, liberal, Republican, Democrat, New Yorker, or Texan and realign with only Jesus" talk. If the Samaritan woman was still holding her jug, this was when she dropped it.

Jesus had unveiled that He is the living water, and whoever drinks in Him will never thirst again for the things of this world. Complete and abundant satisfaction is found only in Christ, and this can take place on a mountain or in a valley, on Sunday or Wednesday, in Jerusalem or Jersey. By shattering the view that worship is an outward display of ceremonial laws, pre-sermon music, or animal sacrifices, Jesus redefined worship for the Samaritans, Jews, and…everybody.

Worship is not something to do, but rather an attitude and an expression of your heart in relation to God. It is what happens within.

REAL WORSHIP

Like the Samaritan woman, I think many of us misunderstand the concept of worship and the gift of living water. In America, we often associate worship with church attendance, praise music, or a regular Bible study. We attribute worship to *the things we do for God* rather than *our relationship with God*. We allow worship to be part of a checklist rather than a joyful relationship with our Creator.

God cares about the orientation of our hearts above all else. He wants us to experience the fullness of joy in Him. He wants us to love Him and engage with Him. He wants worship to be about a continuous, passionate, focused relationship.

It's not about outward displays. How you worship is simply a reflection of your inner state. For some, worship means raising their hands during a song. But for others, it may mean a weeklong fast, serving at the local children's hospital, baking brownies for the guests at the homeless shelter, playing piano at a nursing home, or helping with the lunch line at an elementary school. Worship often includes sacrificial giving or little moments of time committed to others in invisible ways.

The Greek word for worship in the New Testament is *proskuneó*. This word means having reverence, paying homage, or potentially even kissing someone's hand. In fact, *proskuneó* likely comes from the word for a dog licking its owner's hand!

If you spend any time with me, you'll realize I have an unhealthy infatuation with dogs, especially goldendoodles. My doodle, Bear, is the most loving, faithful, affectionate creature God ever created. You can question my fashion sense or my brand of salsa, but please don't try to convince me that doodles aren't the best. It won't end well.

Even though Jason jokes that Bear is 85 pounds of baby fat, I think my doodle is amazing. When I'm gone, Bear will wait patiently by the back door for me to return. When I'm running errands with him, he sits quietly in the back seat of my car and waits for me to talk to him. You'd think he'd rather run around in the back yard with all the squirrels and rabbits. But oh no. He'd rather be in my presence and lathering me with his affection. In the most literal sense, Bear worships me. And like Bear, who is confident I will return his affection, we can approach the One we worship certain of being loved.

The woman at the well wanted the exact same thing all women want: intimacy. She had been desperately searching for it through five husbands. And if we're being honest, many of us are still searching for it through our husbands, boyfriends, careers, fancy parties, and Prime membership. But the intimacy we want can't be found anywhere except with God.

When the Samaritan woman tried to distract Jesus with all sorts of religion talk, He gracefully brought the conversation back to truth. Jesus told the woman there was no more need for external demonstrations of religion, laws, and ceremonies because He had arrived. And if Christ were audibly speaking with us today, I believe He'd echo this same sentiment by reminding us that salvation isn't dependent on our Sunday school attendance, church dress code, or favorite liturgy. Abundant and complete satisfaction can be found only in a relationship with Him, not in traditions and rituals.

Intimacy is a gift. And when intimacy is broken, life feels as though it's spiraling into chaos. I experience this on a minor scale when Jason and I argue. When we can't connect on some subject, be it small or large, I feel lost and grasp for something firm to hold on to. If intimacy is broken with the Creator of the universe, it's not surprising that many of us are flailing, reaching for any branch that may hold peace and purpose.

The greatest part about the story of the woman at the well is that Jesus was persistent about getting through to her. No amount of mistakes, shame, confusion, or heartbreak would stop Him from talking to her. He knew she was a work in progress.

Worshipping Jesus is about becoming. It is a lifelong, sanctifying process of learning to draw from, depend on, and delight in the satisfying waters of God over the broken cisterns of all the lesser things. It is continuously drinking from Christ, the living water. It is growing in intimacy.

THE HEART OF SIBLING RIVALRY

Christmas is my favorite time of year. Lights are everywhere, people are generally happy, and Starbucks offers their limited-time holiday drinks. Most importantly, Jesus is visibly displayed in our home. We have a large nativity scene in our yard, a shiplap board with Isaiah 9:6 hanging above our fireplace, and the Jesse Tree strategically placed on the kitchen counter.

But don't let the scenery fool you. I can get frazzled and anxious. Sometimes the extra holiday hustle and obligations stress me out. To make it worse, sometimes I sense entitlement and discontent in the hearts of my children. Once a few presents start arriving, it's as if the wheels fly right off the car. The conversation morphs into whose present is bigger, better, more expensive, blah, blah, blah.

Last year I adopted a new strategy to help my kids refocus their energy on giving rather than receiving. I gave them various jobs around the house to earn extra spending cash. This money could then be used to buy gifts for their siblings. If they could experience the joy of giving, perhaps it would give them better perspective.

Brilliant, right?

I thought so. Until I took them shopping.

At first, they were all so excited to find that perfect gift and it warmed my heart. But as I watched them shop, I realized something was off. They were searching for the gifts *they* wanted, not the gifts their siblings wanted.

"I'm sorry, Sage, but Reign—your brother who is the walking manifestation of all things sports—is not going to appreciate the pink glitter slime and friendship bracelet. And, Rogue, no, Sage is not going to enjoy 13 different action figures of the Incredible Hulk."

When you say it out loud, it seems obvious. Laughable even. I'm not going to appreciate Jason's new hunting gear from Cabela's, and he's not going to appreciate those two new throw pillows from Magnolia Market. But if I take an honest assessment of my own life and how I worship God, I'm much more like my kids than I want to admit.

I want to attend a church service in the mid-to-late morning hours, so that I have time to get up, enjoy my coffee, and not rush to the service.

I want contemporary music played, not too loud and not too soft, so that I can enjoy my time.

I want the sermon to be applicable to my daily life, without too many references to the Old Testament, aligned with three bullet points and done within 35 minutes.

I want to serve the poor and needy, as long as they only need help on Tuesday nights after 6:30 p.m.

I want my kids to have a robust children's ministry with convenient parking and an atmosphere similar to Disney World.

See the problem? We say it is about worshipping God and His glory, but it's often just about me, myself, and I. We want God, as long as He fits within our own desires and expectations.

This selfish approach isn't new. It's been prevalent since the beginning of time, starting in Genesis with Adam and Eve in the garden of Eden, and it's the centerpiece of the story around Cain and Abel. If you remember your Old Testament history, Cain and Abel were the sons of Adam and Eve. Sin had already entered the world, and the family was no longer in the garden of Eden.

Since sin was now a problem, God began requiring a blood sacrifice, which Cain and Abel would have to fulfill through the slaughtering of one of their flock. (We now know that this was a foreshadowing of what Christ would ultimately do on the cross for all of our sins.) Abel brought the best portions of his flock as an offering, but Cain chose a different approach. He brought an offering, but not of blood. He chose to bring the fruits of the soil. He knew the requirement just like his brother did, but instead, he worshipped God the way he wanted to worship God. He gave God what *he* wanted, not what God required.

Cain's focus wasn't on the Creator. He was thinking about himself. This misplaced worship is a manifestation of a misguided heart. When we depend on self-adequacy over God's sufficiency, when we seek the approval of man over obedience to God, when our minds and schedules are consumed by the things of this world, we demonstrate that God isn't on the throne of our hearts. We are.

God did not accept Cain's offering. Instead, He lovingly warned

Cain that sin was trying to take him down. And how did Cain respond? By killing his brother in overwhelming jealousy.

Misplaced worship will not always lead to physical murder, but it often leads to the death of relationships, dreams, and goals. Self-worship forces us to focus on our accomplishments and instant gratification and sacrifices our intimacy with God. Jesus' example demonstrates that the surrender of self—not the promotion of self—is required to develop healthy relationships and set eternally significant goals. As He prayed in Luke 22:42, "Not my will, but yours be done" (NIV). Jesus trusted the heart of the Father, so His life exemplified a glad surrender of His own will.

When we surrender our desires and dreams to Jesus, we are truly seeking Him first. This is right worship. On the other hand, when we white-knuckle our own agenda, fail to align our plans with His Word, and chase our own glory, we will inevitably hustle down the wrong path and miss the very heart of God, which exhausts our souls. Instead of chasing perfection in ourselves, we need to chase the Perfection of Jesus.

What culture fails to realize is that self-care sometimes stems from deeper-rooted self-worship. Instead of relying on God's character and promises, we try to self-care our way into the perfect little life. We rely on a massage over God's message. We depend on mood-altering exercise instead of heart-altering service to others. We drink from the bottle instead of the Word. These things will never completely satisfy because they were never designed to. The real problem is misdirected worship with a misguided heart. Self-worship chases earthly perfection, but God-worship chases eternal perfection, through a relationship with Christ.

When our motivation for worship isn't driven by a deep desire to know and love God, we will not only worship the wrong things, but we will worship the wrong way. Without the passionate zeal and fervent desire the Holy Spirit brings to our soul, our worship is merely academic assent or legalistic adherence to a set of rules. We cannot usher in the Holy Spirit's work in our lives. This gift is by and through the grace and mercy that is placed upon us from the heavenly Father. Our job is simply to surrender to His promptings, plead for a desire to delight in Him alone, and prepare our hearts to receive His blessings.

John Piper says it magnificently: "Conversion is a set of new desires, not just new duties, new treasures, or new tasks,"[1] and "The essence of praising Christ is prizing Christ."[2] To worship God in spirit, we must treasure and prize Him above everything else. When we love Him with our everything, our new hearts will desire to follow Him in obedience. We will want to be Christlike, holy in our conduct, words, and actions. The other things that compete for our affections will lose their appeal.

My kids can be misguided and selfish. But so can I. And so was Cain. And you probably can be too. Because of God's grace, however, we can start afresh and learn how to worship the One who matters.

TO WORSHIP IS BETTER

The apostle Paul was a ninja when it comes to spiritual issues. In a quiet and powerful way, he sliced directly to truth and left his listeners stunned and amazed.

For example, in Philippians 1:21-23, Paul stated, "To live is Christ and to die is gain. If I am to live in the flesh, that means fruitful labor for me. Yet which I shall choose I cannot tell. I am hard pressed between the two. My desire is to depart and be with Christ, for that is far better."

Paul started his rhetorical debate with a question the rest of us never ask ourselves: Should we live or should we die? At first glance this seems too ridiculous to answer. It's like asking, should we get a massage or strep throat? Finish the pizza or the laundry?

But Paul was anchored to a deep truth. He realized that if he continued to live, he could encourage believers, help strengthen their faith, and expand God's footprint on earth. But if he was to die, he could praise God face-to-face forever. In other words, *to live was to encourage others momentarily, but to die was to worship Christ eternally*. And he knew it was better to worship God.

There are huge implications when we grasp this truth. When we do, we can be extraordinarily brave—forgive the unforgivable, face suffering with unexplainable hope, give grace to the undeserving, listen to the hurting, feed the hungry, hold agendas loosely, share with the needy, and put others' needs—even our enemies—ahead of our own.

If these things sound foreign, it's because we often focus on ourselves, not Jesus. It's counterintuitive, but when Christ is the center of worship, all other things fall into place. You don't have to worry about owning your hustle, driving for success, or building your own kingdom. You don't have to be defined and exhausted by your performance. You can live with joy and peace.

Before Paul's encounter with Jesus on the road to Damascus, Paul was a slave. He was a slave to the law, a slave to performance, a slave to perfection, a slave to other's opinions, and a slave to his culture. But Jesus opened Paul's heart-eyes when He shut his physical eyes. And it gave him clarity and a mission to build God's kingdom, not his own.

When Paul began to worship Jesus—to live for Christ's agenda and not his own—he was truly set free. The soul shackles came off. Likewise, the more we refocus our worship toward God, the more *we will be set free and find rest* for our souls. There will be less fighting over dinner plans, anxiety over work presentations, stressing over weight gain, and longing for approval from the opposite sex.

I'm not downplaying the difficulties of life. It can be hard. Incurable diseases will get a foothold. Good kids will develop addictions. Viruses will become pandemics. Spouses will wander. Markets will crash. Loved ones will die. But the hope we have in Christ Jesus is greater than all these things. We have a greater hope than the world has because Jesus said He would be with us and never leave us (Deuteronomy 31:6). He will right all wrongs (Colossians 3:25). He will restore all that sin has broken (2 Peter 3:13). Our relationship will be fully restored and our eternity forever secured in and through Jesus (Ephesians 4:30; Romans 8:38-39). He will wipe away every tear, and all things will be made new (Revelation 21:4; Romans 8:22-23). We have hope because the joy set before us allows us to endure the pain all around us (Hebrews 12:2).

As I write this I am headed back to my kids. I've been out of the country for the week and I am dying to see them. I miss their faces, their laughs, their funny stories, and yes, even their annoying conflicts. I miss everything about them. I miss when they aren't a part of my day-to-day, when I can't give them a quick hug, exchange a smile, or ask them a question.

The reason I miss them is because I know them. I've spent time with them. I've watched them grow, and I've taken pleasure in nurturing, guiding, and training them. We've played superheroes, made slime, baked cookies, jumped on the trampoline, and watched movies together. We prayed, sang, and cried together. We've spent time together. This is how a *knowing* relationship is built.

God feels the same way about us. But He does it even better. He knows us better than we know our kids. He knows the hairs on our head and is "acquainted with all [our] ways" (Psalm 139:3). When we worship Him, we get to spend time with Him. And in return, we get to experience His love, peace, joy, and desire to be with us as well. When nothing is more important than your relationship with Christ, nothing else compares.

The only question is whether you want to be with Him. Do you want to make Him your heart's desire and top priority? Do you want to worship Him? Or do you want to continue to chase peace on your own? If you have trusted Jesus as Lord of your life and still find yourself with a desire to know Him more, don't stop seeking Him. There will be seasons that feel more dry, that require more discipline and diligence. Jesus said to knock and the door would be opened for you. Seek and He will be found (Matthew 7:7). Draw near to Him and He will draw near to you (James 4:8). Even when it feels more like discipline and less like delight, trust that when you turn to Him, your relationship will grow and fruit will blossom.

Everything in this life, both good and bad, does not compare to knowing and resting in Jesus. Paul knew this. You can too.

AWAKENED HEARTS

Some of us are going through hard things right now. We feel exhausted. Our hearts are dry. Our souls are restless. Our hope is gone.

Fortunately, God is in the business of speaking life back into death.

Ezekiel the prophet was taken by the Spirit to a valley of very dry, dead bones. God told him to speak to those dead bones...and they would come alive. So he did. And immediately flesh began to appear on the bones and they came together. They had form, but they had no breath in them. Then God did what only God can do.

He breathed life into them.

Calling together the four winds, God whispered and spoke life back into the dead body. Left to our own accord, we are bones and flesh and mind, but we have no life in us. But God is able to make all things new again.

In Ezekiel 36:26-27, God said, "I will give you a new heart and put a new spirit in you; I will remove from you your heart of stone and give you a heart of flesh. And I will put my Spirit in you and move you to follow my decrees" (NIV).

Notice that God puts His Spirit in you not so that you can go do whatever you want—but so that you can walk in His ways. So that you can worship and love Him forever.

Those bones that came together after Ezekiel spoke to them have something in common with our hearts. They appear to have life, but they are void of meaning. Until God breathes into them.

And this is exactly what He wants to do when you worship Him.

After meeting Jesus, the Samaritan woman was transformed. Although she was an outcast and didn't interact with the others in the town, she quickly went back and told everyone about Jesus. As you can imagine, they wanted to know more.

So Jesus came and stayed with them for two days. And many others became believers as well. They were all changed. They were all transformed. They were all made new.

Our God is remarkable. And unpredictable. And unbelievably kind to us when we don't deserve it. He is a God worth worshipping.

4

An Uncomfortable Truth

If you abide in my word, you are truly
my disciples, and you will know the
truth, and the truth will set you free.

JOHN 8:31-32

We all have that one brave friend. You know, the bungee-jumping, motorcycle-riding, tornado-chasing, hang-gliding friend who needs less than 30 seconds to make a life-changing decision. Actually, I have a few. These are my "ready, fire, aim" friends. They aim for the target after they've already cut loose. Without these slightly unbalanced friends, I wouldn't have done half the crazy things I can now brag about.

One of my brave friends is currently living in Texas, my home away from home. I have always admired her zest and passion for adventure. One day she called me and asked if I'd like to try something new and exciting. Before I had a chance to ask about mortality rates or update my will, she had me committed.

She told me it was called stand-up paddleboarding, also known as SUP. I didn't know much about this "extreme" sport at the time. All I knew was that it involved water, a board, and a paddle. And it seemed a bit edgy and cool. It was definitely outside my typical, dull, go-for-a-long-run exercise routine.

I had seen pictures of women much older than me on their boards gracing the pages of the Athleta catalog. They made it look easy. Not to mention, they were often accompanied by their adorable canine companions. So how difficult could it be? I wasn't going to be skydiving in a foreign country or hot-air ballooning across the Atlantic. And I like to push myself. I've run a half marathon in the scorching heat of August and done a backflip on a four-inch balance beam. Paddleboarding seemed like a half step forward without leaping into the unknown.

Now, you should know something about me that I'm not particularly proud of. I'm a recovering people pleaser and a little competition obsessed. As you can imagine, this can get me into trouble at times. My brave friend doesn't help when it comes to this. I think she knows my weaknesses and works it to her advantage.

Besides, I had already been imagining Hawaiian-like beaches and me gracefully gliding across serene, clear, emerald waters. As the sun glistened off my bare shoulders and hair perfectly set in a topknot, I could only imagine that Jason would be glad he married me. And this scene would make some pretty killer pictures for Instagram as well. Not that anyone considers such a thing.

When I arrived for the first SUP class in the less serene lake waters of Texas, I immediately knew my mental picture had been a bit miscalculated. There were approximately 20 women gathered and ready to board. They had all the right gear—their *own* gear—boards and paddles and other equipment with which I was unfamiliar. I was given an old rental board that looked as though it had been rebuilt from the *Mayflower*. And everyone had life belts. What kind of gentle activity on the water requires a belt for saving your life?! The thought may have made me pee my pants a little. Good thing we were getting in the water.

And did I mention it was windy? Not a cool breeze kind of windy, but rather an "eating my hair and trying to capsize the *Titanic*" windy. My friend forgot to tell me the wind may be a slight problem. I was told the class would cancel if winds reached 18 miles an hour. But as I looked around, no one with any meteorological experience was monitoring the gusts. They were just strapping on more safety gear.

As I slowly approached the rocky bank to get on my clunky, beat-up board, I watched the others kneel and then gracefully stand up on their boards while pushing away from the shore. They made it look so effortless. Perhaps I had a chance.

As I mounted the board, I stumbled around like a geriatric ostrich, tipping, tottering, and nearly falling backward into six feet of water. But I made it up. I could feel my heart beating so hard I thought it would come out of my throat. Or maybe it was the Starbucks I had on the way to class.

At this point the others were so far down the lake I could barely see them. I took the paddle in my hands and began fighting the angry waves. When I finally escaped the undercurrent and hurricane gusts, I looked up just in time to see the bridge. Within a moment, I was tumbling backward and into the water—the board flying in one direction and the paddle in the other. Fortunately, my life belt was still attached, but for better or worse, it didn't inflate.

I must've been a sight.

Beyond embarrassed, I quickly swam back to my board. The instructor paddled toward me, waiting to see if I was all right and pouring out words of encouragement. She must have been laughing under her breath.

My hair was wet and messy, makeup and muddy lake water were pasted over my cheeks, and I was clearly not getting the tan I was expecting. This moment was definitely not social media worthy. As we made our way back to dry land, we began to regroup and reassess.

At this point the instructor said the winds were too strong to keep going. Captain Obvious told me it was better to call it a day and try again next week.

My first thought was, *Come back? Are you kidding me?! I'd rather run barefoot over broken glass or roll around in poison ivy.* So I did what any sane and normal person would do.

I came back.

And guess what? That summer turned out to be a blast, and I grew to love the sport. Sadly, it wasn't the last time I fell off the board. But I knew if I played it safe, I would never improve. Growth comes at a cost. The experience taught me grit and resolve, and it made the glory of building relationships and staying dry all the richer.

Our hearts are much like paddleboards. We assume they don't do well in the wind and on the waves. We think they are made for calm and settled waters. So we stay on the land we know and stick to the things we recognize.

But the opposite is actually true. When we live through turbulent, chaotic times and when our hearts are thrashed by circumstances, we thrive and grow the most. We were made to do hard things, and in the storm when it feels as if we are going to drown, we begin to look for our life belt. We begin to look for Jesus.

THE ANCHOR

Growing up in the Midwest was a good thing for me. You can find wonderful people all over our beautiful country, but I learned a great deal by being surrounded by humble people who loved without pretense and lived with deep fortitude. In my biased opinion, Kansans are the salt of the earth.

My father and grandfather were both wheat farmers. In the fall, my sister and I would ride the combines during harvest. I remember wearing overalls and braiding each other's hair. I also remember the dusty fields, large plots of land that were replete with acres and acres of wheat that had been delicately sown the spring before.

My great-grandparents lived in a tiny farmhouse across from these wheat fields. Next to the farmhouse was an old barn. Everyone had a barn. In preparation for the Kansas winter, farmers would tie a rope from their back door of the farmhouse to the inside of the barn. Blizzards would sometimes produce what is known as a "whiteout," a storm so intense it was impossible to see more than a few feet. When there were no visual points of reference from which to navigate, the rope would help farmers find their way to and from the barn, saving them from freezing to death. The rope was their anchor to safety, their guide back home.

As believers, we often find ourselves caught in the storms of life where we have little visibility and no guidance. We have marriages that are falling apart, children who are falling away, and promises that are falling through. At these times, we too need an Anchor to survive the treacherous circumstances.

In the first century, Christians were persecuted and martyred beyond anything we in the United States can imagine today. They were beaten, tortured, thrown to the ravenous lions, and even burned at the stake. Roman emperor Nero was a ruthless leader, set on taking down and destroying the followers of Christ, or followers of The Way.

To encourage one another discreetly, these early Christians secretly used the symbol of an anchor to declare solidarity to the cause of Christ. You can find anchor marks on countless tombstones in the St. Domitilla and Priscilla cemeteries to this day. It's an interesting observation that the top of the anchor's shape is similar to a cross, a visual representation of Christ's sacrifice.

Even today we see the anchor displayed as a symbol throughout our culture. We wear them around our necks, print them on our coffee mugs, and even tattoo them on our wrists. But more than anything, we desperately need the anchor engraved on our hearts.

On its own, the heart is restless. It flounders. It wavers and waffles. It's desperately sick and needs help. It doesn't need to be followed—it needs to be informed. It needs to commit and trust God. It aimlessly rides the waves of our busy lives, desperately trying to cling to something deeper and stronger.

The anchor is what steadies the vessel. Our hearts may be battered by the waves of circumstance, but the anchor holds it secure and safe. We will still be battered by the waves, but the anchor will ultimately keep us from crashing against the rocks.

If you feel unmoored right now, you are not alone. Even as I write this, I'm wrestling with my commitment to ministry and parenting my kids. This tension of juggling these important commitments feels erratic and chaotic at times. I often wonder if I'm encouraging other women and families at the cost of my own. Perhaps you feel the same about your kids or spouse or singleness or career or just overall direction and purpose. Our circumstances may be different, but the storm is the same.

There will be times when we let our agendas rule our hearts, control our peace, and distract our purpose. And no weekly manicure, exercise program, or color-coded calendar will anchor you. You'll need something much more reliable.

Mary knew this. Which was why she sat at Jesus' feet, captivated by every word that flowed from the Savior's lips. The Samaritan woman knew it as well. Despite living in disgrace and apart from community, she ran and told everyone she knew about this Jesus and what He had shared with her. In both instances, Jesus was revealing that He is the truth and we are called to worship in truth. And this truth affects both our hearts and our minds.

Without truth on our hearts, we run the risk of worshipping the right thing in the wrong way. Without truth in our minds, we run the risk of worshipping the wrong thing in the right way.

Truth is the anchor.

SO WHAT IS TRUTH?

This is an important question with an even more important answer. If we are called to worship God in truth, we need to understand what it is. Our understanding, or lack thereof, will have huge implications on our lives.

Our postmodern culture would like us to believe that there is no such thing as absolute truth. They believe there are no right or wrong answers—everything is just a matter of perspective and opinion. But to say there is no absolute truth is to make an absolute statement, which contradicts itself.

Consider a bottle of water. A bottle of water cannot be both a bottle of water and a bowl of cereal at the same time. It's nonsensical. This is called the law of noncontradiction. If two differing views both claim to be true, one has to be false. Yet culture is attempting to promote the idea that contradictory situations can both be true.

For example, some people believe a person's sex is determined by their chromosomes and others believe it is something you can choose. Both can't be right. Some religions believe women are the property of their husbands, and some religions (Christianity) believe all people are equal under God. Both can't be right.

We could go on and on, but I think you get the point. An objective, eternal truth must exist outside of our own personal feelings or we will spiral into utter chaos.

Many embrace this new age ideology, marked by subjective relativism. Your truth, my truth, his truth, her truth—anything goes. However, we are not the first society to tread down this path of extreme individualism. Judges 17:6 states that in the time of the judges, "Everyone did what was right in his own eyes." Turn on any television station or view any popular social media channel and you'll hear the same thing: do what you feel is right for you.

And therein lies the problem.

Too many people, including professing Christians, believe they can do whatever feels right to them. This is contradictory to the gospel of Jesus Christ. If you believe the biblical God is God, then you have to accept that "whoever wants to be [Jesus Christ's] disciple must deny themselves and take up their cross and follow [Him]" (Matthew 16:24 NIV).

The reason we are talking about truth at all right now is because too many women are not anchoring themselves to the truth of the Bible. We are easily swayed by the opinions of the world and the pressures of culture. Even among professing believers, there is a "progressive Christianity" movement, which, when studied, is not Christianity at all. It embraces universal and pluralistic ideologies, and its teachings are subtle and deceptive. The only way we are going to be able to discern what is right and wrong is if we dedicate ourselves to studying God's Word.

This is where I'm going to lose some of you. This is where some of you who just want a feel-good message or a short list of things to fix are going to close the book. This is where some of you start thinking you've heard all this before. This is where some of you go back to doing whatever you want. My prayer is that you don't give up now—stay with me. Let's walk this out together and see what goodness God has for us on the other side.

C.H. Spurgeon has been credited with saying, "Discernment is not knowing the difference between right and wrong, but knowing the difference between right and almost right." Most of the decisions you have to make on a daily basis aren't between right and wrong. Should you sleep with your husband or the next-door neighbor? Should you eat a balanced diet or have a bag of Cheetos for lunch? Should you charge a thousand dollars on your credit card that you can't repay or live within your means? These are all relatively easy to answer because the line between right and wrong is obvious.

But the enemy is crafty when he tempts us. There is nothing wrong with signing up for that spin class, taking the promotion at work, or taking care of your home, is there? It depends. Does that spin class overlap with the few hours you have with your kids? Does that promotion take important time away from your husband and his needs? Does making your home beautiful overshoot your budget and stress your family?

The world doesn't ask these questions because they expose our sinful nature and remind us of the truth. And what is the truth?

Just Jesus—the way, the truth, and the life (John 14:6). We have to start with Him.

REVISITING TRUTH

John 1:1-4 says, "In the beginning was the Word, and the Word was with God, and the Word was God…All things were made through him, and without him was not anything made that was made. In him was life, and the life was the light of men."

Jesus described Himself as the Word.

This verse used to confuse me. How could Jesus be a word? How could He be the actual Bible? It didn't make sense until I learned about the word in Greek, *logos*.

Logos means the complete, revealed message and full expression of God. It describes the totality and fulfillment of a message. So when the Bible reveals Jesus as the *Logos*, it is referring to the full embodiment of God and His eternal plan.

Another way to understand the Word as *logos* is the idea of expression. The Bible is the written expression of the message lived out in the life of Jesus Christ. His story of redemption and love, God's glory revealed through the person of Jesus and His work of salvation through His death on the cross, is beautifully woven in and throughout the entirety of Scripture.

The *logos*, or the message of Jesus, are the building blocks of Scripture. Like the DNA in our bodies, it is encoded in every letter that is written. Every story and every passage reveals or points to Jesus and the gospel message. The Old Testament predicts and foreshadows, while the New Testament reveals and fulfills. Jesus is in the DNA of the Bible.

Why is all this important? Because Jesus is the foundation and ultimate truth revealed throughout Scripture. Without Christ as the cornerstone and centerpiece, we are just reading a bunch of confusing stories and interesting history.

This is why we don't do ourselves any favors when we cherry-pick verses throughout the Bible. We miss the bigger picture, the greater narrative. Too many of us are opening the Bible to a random page, hoping God will shine a spotlight on that one special verse we need to hear while the eternal choir of angels sings "Hallelujah!" While possible, this doesn't seem to be God's preferred approach to revealing truth.

Jen Wilkin, an author and teacher, calls this the "Xanax approach" to Scripture reading. When we are anxious and distracted, just pop a verse of Scripture and a warm dose of feel-good should settle the soul. She goes on to say that for many of us, "devotional reading is like chamomile tea—a soothing drink before slumber. No one drinks chamomile tea before going to war. We need stronger drink to combat the world, the flesh, and the devil. We need battle cries as well as lullabies. We need the full counsel of Scripture."[1] When God illuminates the *logos* and you submit to the beauty and love of the gospel, you can't help but see and experience this undeniable truth.

In addition to *logos*, another Greek word that is often used for the Word in the Bible is *rhema*. In John 6:60-71, Jesus asked Peter if he would like to walk away from Him, as many other followers had done. Peter responded, "Lord, to whom shall we go? You have the words [*rhema*] of eternal life, and we have believed, and have come to know, that you are the Holy One of God" (verses 68-69).

Paul also referred to *rhema* in Ephesians 6:17-18, when he said to take up the "sword of the Spirit, which is the word [*rhema*] of God, praying at all times in the Spirit" as an offensive weapon used to defeat the enemy.

When reading Scripture, you can easily distinguish between the two. Think of the *logos* as the embodiment of Christ Himself and the broad message of the gospel. And think of *rhema* as the specific sayings of truth that Christ shared. Both are exceptionally important and both are made clear as you explore Scripture. As you read the Bible, ask the Holy Spirit to reveal to you the foundational truth, the *logos*, of Christ and His ministry. It will speak directly to your heart and will drive out confusion, worry, and distraction. And with this newfound peace and purpose, you can then begin to ingest the *rhema* words that empower you to walk boldly.

Friends, we need to dive deep into the Word, pray for ears to hear and eyes to see, and then be still. Let's not miss that last part. His voice is often a small whisper that can only be heard in the depths of a quiet heart. Still the noise and distractions so you can hear and know that He is God.

Losing weight is not the answer. Making money is not the answer. Attaining knowledge is not the answer. Self-care is not the answer. A new relationship is not the answer. Having kids is not the answer. A new job is not the answer. A different church is not the answer.

Jesus is the answer, every single time. Jesus is the Word. The Word is the Truth. And the Truth sets us free.

AN UNCOMFORTABLE TRUTH

The truth is often uncomfortable.

When Jesus was tempted in the desert, I can only imagine how uncomfortable He must have been. We often think of God in His eternal presence and forget about His human experience. But He was all God *and* all human. And in His humanity, He must have been awfully hungry, thirsty, and exhausted in the desert.

Not to mention that He was in the desert for 40 days. I've fasted for three or four days in an air-conditioned house and felt as though I should be awarded the Bronze Star for bravery. I just don't have any real understanding of what it takes to endure such conditions for over a month.

At the end of their training, every marine goes through the Crucible—an agonizing 54-hour event that tests every recruit physically, mentally, and emotionally. They march over 48 miles carrying 45 pounds of gear while enduring 36 challenging obstacles and 29 team-building exercises. The recruits endure extreme amounts of physical fatigue, sleep deprivation, dehydration, and despair. They are pushed to the end of themselves and learn how to lean on one another. Every marine says the experience is both horrendous and transformational, a rite of passage necessary to prepare them to serve and protect others.

Our Savior, Jesus, had to endure in extreme conditions as well. For 40 days, He was without all the necessities of the world. He endured extreme physical, mental, and emotional pain, all the while being tested by the ultimate tempter, Satan. Christ could have called down legions of angels to protect Him, turned the rocks into bread, or just tapped out. But instead, He endured miserable, near life-ending conditions so that He—the Truth incarnate—would be prepared and strengthened for the ministry and mission ahead of Him.

Satan is at work today in our lives just like he was with Jesus in the desert. But he has employed a new and deceptive strategy: make everyone comfortable. He wants to distract us with our fleshly desires. He wants to make our lives so easy that almost anything seems more appealing than following Christ.

I hate to admit it, but I love to shop. It doesn't matter whether it's online or in person. I love pretty things—shoes, purses, and jeans with a perfect fit and fade. I can easily obsess over an adorable Magnolia Market wreath and aviator shades that hide my ever-growing eye wrinkles. And if it isn't shopping, I can be distracted with check-lists, emails, and social media. Even the treadmill in the corner of the basement—which has turned into an expensive clothes rack—sometimes has more appeal than quiet time with Jesus. There are times when loading the dishwasher or folding the laundry feels more urgent and necessary than opening my Bible.

I've gotten comfortable and I'm easily distracted.

But what I've learned is that when my children are fighting, when my heart is hurting, when my husband is distant, none of these comforts can help. Only the truth can. Only the Word of God applied with grace and perseverance can. It breaks chains. It penetrates and goes deep to deal with the root of the problem, not just the symptoms.

As an example, when my children fight, I try to remember that conflicts are an opportunity to demonstrate grace instead of expressing frustration and anger. Jesus put our needs before His when He endured the cross so we can give preference to others as well. He showed self-control in His responses so we can listen before we speak. He forgave our sins so we can forgive others who have wronged us. Truth allows us to see conflicts as opportunities to show and live the gospel.

Truth is like a scalpel in the hand of a surgeon. It can cut deep, but delicately and precisely. It removes that which is deadly so we can be bandaged back up and heal. Truth is not a hatchet that swings wildly and creates collateral damage. And it's not a Band-Aid that tries to cover up a gunshot wound. It is a precise instrument used to get to the heart of the problem.

If you are not experiencing peace and purpose in your life, could it be that you know about God, but you don't really know God?

This is an uncomfortable question that has to be asked. Because our souls don't need more pedicures or beach getaways. We need Jesus. We need to experience Him. We need to see Him high and lifted up. And we need to see Him up close, sitting with us in the mess we created, arms holding us tight and hands catching our tears.

This isn't about head knowledge or better theology. The Devil has deep knowledge of God and is a better theologian than any of us. But he doesn't embrace the truth about Him—that He is ultimately good and wants what is eternally best for all His children.

And the truth about ourselves? It can get uncomfortable because it's personal. Each and every one of us has to embrace or reject the truth about who we are. We must admit that we sin, that we aren't any good on our own, and that we need Jesus. We have to lay down our pride, and dare I say, our own independence. If we truly want to be free, then we have to embrace the hard truth that dependence on God grants internal and eternal freedom.

Jesus claimed the reason He came into the world was to bear witness to the truth and said those who were of the truth would listen to Him. We need to be women "of the truth." Because truth is found in the Word of God, and begins with eyes opened and beholding a proper and right understanding of God through the gospel of Jesus Christ.

TRUTH NEEDS A PLAN

If you haven't heard this message clearly in this chapter so far, let me shout it from the cheap seats: there is no substitute for time in God's Word.

We aren't going to find our hope in our own abilities. We aren't going to find hope in goal setting, self-love, or self-care. We aren't going to find hope in a great job or a great spouse. We aren't even going to find hope in another Bible study or a new church. All of our self-prescribed medications will never give us peace and purpose. Only a personal relationship with Christ and daily nourishment in the Word can guide us.

The reason we are stuck is because we think we are the solution. But when it's all about us, we stay on the failure train. We constantly look for the next big thing, diet, book, fad, or business to make us feel better about ourselves or give us an inkling of hope. But when things don't pan out, our souls fall into anguish.

We must prioritize what matters. While you ultimately can't find purpose with tips and tricks, I do want to discuss a few tactical steps to help you get started spending time in the Word.

1. Make time.

We have to *make time* to meet with Jesus. Notice how I didn't say *find time* or *schedule time*. We have to *make time*. We always make time for what's important to us. If youth theater or date night or working out is important, you will make time for it. Ironically, all these other things hinge off our spiritual health so we have to make sure time with Christ is number one. If this sounds harsh, I can't apologize. This is too important to mince words or soften the blow. We need to lovingly but forcefully be pushed in the right direction, as if our life depended on it...because it does.

If we don't spend time in His Word, we won't understand the truth. And the truth is what sets us free. Second Corinthians 3:17 says that where the Spirit of the Lord is, there is freedom. And when we turn to the Lord (in His Word), we will behold the glory of the Lord and be changed, little by little, from one degree of glory to another. This change comes from the Spirit.

We become what we behold. If we keep looking toward God in His Word, we will become more like Him. Our marriages will be more holy, loving, and life-giving. Our attitudes less grumpy. Our hearts more content and our paths clearer. The strong grasp of sin will be diminished, and we will experience peace that is not tied to our ever-changing circumstances.

If we look to the world, we will more easily fall prey to subtle lies, comparison, and discontent. We will forget our identity and purpose. We will forget His high call and great compassion.

As you think about the time you want to devote to God, I'd encourage you to make time when you are at your best. Your husband doesn't want to have sex with you when you are exhausted and you lie there motionless. Neither does God want your second best or your leftovers. He wants you to be focused, passionate, and on fire for what He is about to show you.

> The Lord isn't in the Facebook notifications, the laundry cycles, the board meetings, or the traffic jams. He is the gentle whisper that follows.

I've found my best is in the morning, after a good night of sleep. Not only am I more rested, but if I get up early, people are not vying for my attention and time. I can be consistent. Moreover, it helps tremendously to prepare my heart and mind for the day that is coming. I can handle Bear pooping on the floor and Jason taking a last-minute dinner meeting better when I've centered myself on the Word in the morning.

But if the morning doesn't work for you, then make time when you can focus and be quiet. I promise He will blow your mind in the ways He will move and work through this daily discipline. You will soon find that you can't live without it. As hunger for food and thirst for water, your soul will crave this time of refilling.

2. Have a plan.

As mentioned earlier, don't play Bible roulette—don't just randomly open up the Bible and hope for the best. Have a plan. Hundreds of good resources are available, both online and in physical formats, that can help you delve into the Word of God. I won't list them all out here, but if you'd like a little more guidance, I've listed my favorite tools and resources at www.alishaillian.com.

For the last few years, I've personally enjoyed reading through the Bible chronologically to grasp God's big picture. I don't rush through it.

I take my time. And if I find something particularly interesting during one of my readings, I stop and do a little more homework. The Read Scripture app has a plan that also includes a daily psalm and the Bible Project videos to help visual learners like me with specific concepts that can be difficult to understand.

3. Slow down.

Hurry drowns out the voice of God. And we are always in a hurry. Whether we are rushing to pick up the kids, get dinner on the table, or prepare for a meeting, we are running 100 miles per hour with our hair on fire.

Slow down.

Life wasn't meant to be endured, and Scripture isn't meant to be consumed at breakneck speeds. It's meant to be prayed through, contemplated, meditated, and studied. It's meant to be responded to. It's a conversation. It speaks to the deepest parts of our souls. It's not a race to a finish line. It's a relationship that needs to be nurtured and enjoyed.

If you are eating a fantastic dinner, you don't try to eat faster to enjoy it more. Just the opposite. You slow down. You take it all in. The same can be said of our daily manna, the Word of God. Let it nourish and revive your soul. Let it guide your thoughts. So slow down and enjoy what God is teaching you.

TRUTH NEEDS QUIET SPACE

I have several unique habits that entertain Jason. When I am driving somewhere unfamiliar and need to focus, I turn down the radio. I don't know if it's my ADD brain or a lack of sleep, but I can't seem to focus when there is too much stimulus. Jason doesn't understand how a quiet car can help my eyesight, but I insist it makes a big difference.

While I can't explain the science behind my overstimulation, I can confirm there is power in quiet moments. Multiple times throughout Jesus' ministry He gets away from the crowds and the disciples to find a quiet place. As Mark 1:35 puts it, "Early in the morning, while it was still dark, Jesus got up and slipped out to a solitary place to pray" (BSB). Even Jesus realized there was too much noise and distraction. And if the Creator of the universe needs time to rest, pray, and seek silence, I'm certain we need it as well.

When Elijah was running for his life in 1 Kings 19:11-13, he was anxious and confused about all that was going on around him. So the Lord instructed Elijah to go stand alone on the mountain in the presence of the Lord until He passed by.

> Then a great and powerful wind tore the mountains apart and shattered the rocks before the LORD, but the LORD was not in the wind. After the wind there was an earthquake, but the LORD was not in the earthquake. After the earthquake came a fire, but the LORD was not in the fire. And after the fire came a still, small voice (BSB).

The Lord wasn't in the wind, the earthquake, or the fire. He was the still, small voice that Elijah had to strain to focus on and hear amid the noise and madness. The same can be said in our daily lives. The Lord isn't in the Facebook notifications, the laundry cycles, the board meetings, or the traffic jams. He is the gentle whisper that follows. But to hear it, we have to quiet our hearts and lives. Jesus escaped the hustle and bustle of His own ministry—which we can argue may be the most important work ever done on earth—to spend quiet time with His Father. We need to do the same.

When I finally learned to paddleboard, I discovered that I made no progress if my paddle just skimmed the surface of the water. To get traction, I needed to completely submerge my paddle deep into the water. I needed to be consistent in my rhythm and I needed to reach and pull.

It was hard work, but soon I was paddling with the best of them. I still have the occasional fall, but I've learned to enjoy the beauty of the struggle and I now know that it will ultimately make me stronger.

Every once in a while I'll still get caught off guard by a strong moving storm or some violent current. I'm often tempted to panic when I see the waves or hear the thunder. It's usually when I'm just about to give up and give in when I hear a still small voice say…

"Keep paddling, brave friend. Keep paddling."

5

Brave Fear

I sought the Lord, and he answered
me and delivered me from all my fears.
Those who look to him are radiant, and
their faces shall never be ashamed.

PSALM 34:4-5

When I was four, I remember having my first dream. It all started during the 1984 summer Olympics. If you were alive at that time, you know what I'm talking about. Every proud American was fixated on their pixilated TV screen as the sweet and spunky American gymnast, Mary Lou Retton, stepped up to the vault.

She was only four foot nine, but what she did made her a giant that day. With heart and passion, she landed a perfect 10 on the vault, earning herself a gold medal and catapulting her into instant stardom. Not only did she stick the landing, but she also stuck a dream deep into my heart. From that day on, I wanted to become an Olympic gymnast more than anything else.

I will save you the suspense and tell you that I never made it to the

Olympics. But I did compete in gymnastics at a high level for many years. As I got older, however, my genetics began to work against me. I became a gorilla in a room full of monkeys. Having some height is great if you are a model or a basketball player, but it makes all the acrobatic moves in the gym that much harder.

One practice remains etched in my memory. I was standing behind a teammate, waiting for her to finish her routine on the uneven bars. She was working on a difficult move, a blind release, that would take her from the high bar over the low bar. As she swung backward, her hands slipped off the bar. Panicked, she tried to break the fall with her arms but ultimately landed on her face, experiencing the worst of both gravity and geometry. She fell so hard and so fast that her arm literally snapped in half and was bent 90 degrees in the wrong direction.

When I realized what had happened, I yelled for help and ran straight for the nearest coach. Before I knew it, my teammate was carried off in an ambulance, with sirens echoing throughout the facility. Up to this point, I'd always worked hard and enjoyed the sport. But for the first time I experienced fear. Real, unbridled fear.

At the time of the freak accident, I had been working on one of the most important moves a gymnast can perform on the high bar. It's known as the Giant. It's a big name for a big move.

If you've ever watched gymnastics, you've seen the Giant. It's when the gymnast strikes a handstand on a lone tall bar and then swings faster and faster around the bar in a full circle, fully extended and without letting go. It takes incredible forearm and grip strength. It's the move that makes skydivers blush and the one that takes ten years off your mom's life.

I had no problem performing this move when the coach was standing there spotting me. But as soon as he stepped back, I became paralyzed with fear. I couldn't make it all the way around the bar. I knew my struggle wasn't physical—it was the mental part that had me all tangled up inside.

Unfortunately, I've experienced fear like this many times in my life. I've been afraid of not getting into college, and then scared about not succeeding when I got there. I've been afraid of being single forever, and then even more afraid of not being a good enough wife once I got married. I was afraid we couldn't have kids, and then terrified when I had to figure out how to parent them.

The one common thread in nearly all my bouts with fear is that it was unwarranted. Fear is debilitating and frightening, but it is never necessary. I just allow the loud negative voices in my head to drown out God's confidence. I let fear overwhelm my faith.

We all have different coping mechanisms, but my go-to is *control.* When I sense fear is rising, I try to take control of the situation. For some reason, I have this false belief that I can white-knuckle control away from the problem with sheer force. Of course, it never works. More control never mastered any giants in our life, or when it comes to gymnastics, the Giant.

When I was frightened on the high bar, no pep talk or happy memory was going to release the sense of fear I had. So instead of overcoming it, I had to go through it. After numerous failed attempts, I willed my legs to move and finally gained enough speed to get all the way around. It was ugly at first, but I did it. So then I tried again. And the process grew easier. As I began to relinquish control, fear was released, my body became less stiff, and I started to regain a sense of rhythm and grace.

I learned something important that day. Courage isn't a lack of fear—it's moving forward in spite of it. It's going in scared. It's not waiting for fear to leave, permission to be granted, approval given, or the way to be clear. It's moving in fear, moving in doubt, and moving despite inadequacy and inability. It's moving forward, often awkwardly, but bravely. You have to go through it. You have to make mistakes and keep pressing on.

Faith and fear are connected but have a negative correlation. As

> Courage isn't a lack of fear—it's moving forward in spite of it. It's going in scared.

faith wanes, fear rises. But as faith rises, fear gives way to boldness. As Ann Voskamp notes, "Fear is what we feel—but brave is what we do."[1]

Sisters, brave is what we do. We can be brave not because we are the hero of our own story but because Christ has already claimed victory. When others are flailing in relationships and in their purpose, we can hold firmly to Him who has taken a firm hold on us. Moving forward without guarantees is a reflection of a growing faith. And this is the fertile ground that births the brave that moves mountains…and Giants.

ANXIOUS FOR NOTHING

Anxiety disorders are the most common mental illness in the United States, affecting over 40 million adults. That's basically one out of every five of us. To make matters worse, women are twice as likely to be affected. So, ladies, this is kind of our thing.

Even more alarming, anxiety is often linked to depression. This means many of us are living worried, scared, and perpetually sad. Fear is a constant joy stealer because we cannot thrive in a perpetual state of worry. There are times that anxiety and depression are a result of physiological chemical imbalances or hormonal influences, but when our worries are attached to a fundamental distrust of God, they can become a debilitating sin struggle.

When we allow worry to dominate our thoughts, we are listening to lies. Lies told me I wouldn't make it over the high bar, and lies told me I would get hurt. But none of that was founded on the truth. Lies are a breeding ground for fear, so we have to combat the fear with God's eternal truths. Truth builds a gritty faith and arms us to brave fear. So let's take in some truth.

In this chapter I want to challenge you to read every Scripture verse below out loud. I don't care if you are with your kids, your friends, your coworkers, or the guy fixing your furnace. They need to hear it too. Speak boldly and hear God's promises. They will combat the lying voices in your head.

Let's start with Philippians 4:4-9:

> Rejoice in the Lord always. I will say it again: Rejoice! Let your graciousness be known to everyone. The Lord is near. Don't worry about anything, but in everything, through prayer and petition with thanksgiving, present your requests to God. And the peace of God, which surpasses all understanding, will guard your hearts and minds in Christ Jesus.
>
> Finally brothers and sisters, whatever is true, whatever is honorable, whatever is just, whatever is pure, whatever is lovely, whatever is commendable—if there is any moral excellence and if there is anything praiseworthy—dwell on these things. Do what you have learned and received and heard from me, and seen in me, and the God of peace will be with you (csb).

Okay, now slow down and read it again…out loud.

Consider the context of the passage. Paul was addressing two women who were in a major tiff. And this conflict must've been causing them great anxiety. They were also women of faith, fully devoted to Jesus and the ministry. So Paul could have been talking about you and your sister, you and your mother, you and your best friend, or you and another believer in Christ. The point is that our current flesh struggles are not unique. We are all on a journey and must daily surrender our passions and relinquish control to realign our hearts. Just like these gals in Philippi needed some encouragement and counsel, we need it in spades in our own lives. Reflecting on the passage, here are the important elements to think about:

1. Rejoice, rejoice.

Paul started out with this unlikely command—*rejoice.* Actually, he said it twice, which means we should probably pay attention.

Repetition is a clue that something is important or urgent. My seven-year-old is an expert when it comes to applying attention-getting repetition. In fact, corporations and government entities should pay him for his expertise. When I'm on the phone, chatting with a friend, or squatting quietly on the porcelain throne, he often starts the repetitious chatter of, "Mom! Mom! Mom!," "Hey, hey, hey," or any other combination of annoying sounds to get my attention. The more private and personal my activity, the more pressing and persistent he becomes. Paul would be proud.

The Greek word for rejoice is *chairo*, which means to thrive, be glad, be well-off, or be calmly happy. I like that—calmly happy. Instead of being highly emotional, ecstatically happy, and bouncing off the walls, *chairo* refers to an inner, soul-peace happy. It's happy like "a mother rocking her sleeping baby on the porch while sipping on an ice-cold glass of sweet tea" happy. Calm and happy.

While that sounds nice, it seems impractical in many instances, right? In this situation, Paul was trying to break up a catfight between two women in Philippi, and calm happiness seemed miles away. But since "rejoice" is being specifically attached to "in the Lord," Paul was sharing some wisdom. While it may be impossible for us to be calmly happy on our own in the toughest of circumstances, we can find this inner peace *in the Lord.*

2. Remember the Lord is near.

Paul wanted to remind us that we are not alone. The Lord is near. In our lives, it often feels as though God is abstract and distant, but our feelings are misleading. Robert Murray M'Cheyne once said, "If I could hear Christ praying for me in the next room, I would not fear a million enemies. Yet the distance makes no difference; he is praying for me."[2]

The Lord is near. He is personal. He is caring.

We need to trust that the Lord is close by, fighting for us and working through us. The more we know of God, the more we trust and experience His presence, the smaller our problems will become. The more we know of His unchanging character and holiness, the heavier our sin will feel. This disturbing revelation should draw us closer to God, where we can experience His truly amazing grace. At this time we find that He isn't millions of miles away—He's been with us all along.

The Lord is near, and He shows up in many different ways in our lives.

I challenge you to look up all the different names of God in the Bible. These names—Elohim, El Shaddai, Adonai, and more—are a reflection of all His various characteristics and unchanging nature. If you are having trouble finding His names, feel free to go to www.alishaillian .com and check out the list I've provided. If you keep this list in your Bible, post it on your bathroom mirror, or make it the screensaver on your phone, you'll be reminded of God's presence. Pray through those names. Let them be engraved on your heart and imprinted on your soul.

3. Pray about everything...with thanksgiving.

Bedtime prayers with my kids can turn into a mindless echo chamber of praying for "a fun time, a good day, and a wonderful family." If their prayers seem shallow, it's because *they* are—and because the kids learned this behavior from us.

God told us we should pray about everything. And if He tells us this, then He must care immensely about all the details and worries of our lives. You may be tempted to leave out the struggle you are having with your sister, the hours of time you are wasting on social media, or your unhealthy focus on your weight. Don't. Share all the details. Fill Him in. Get in the habit of being intimate with Him as you share your needs and concerns. But don't expect to receive resolution for every problem or have your every prayer answered the way you think you need. Prayer isn't about God giving us what we want, but about Him aligning our hearts with His.

Ladies, you know how loved you feel when your husband or a good friend really listens to all the details of your day and all the concerns of your heart. It fills up your love tank. God does this even better. He doesn't have a bad day, and He doesn't get distracted by SportsCenter. He isn't too bored or too busy. He actually looks forward to you sharing both your excitement and your sadness.

Second Chronicles 16:9 states, "The eyes of the LORD run to and fro throughout the whole earth, to give strong support to those whose heart is blameless toward him." In other words, He is actively looking for those who want to spend time with Him. He wants to support and bless you.

And when you pray, do so with thanksgiving. God may not make a sickness go away or save you or a loved one from a terrible situation, but He has promised to stay near to you. Even when we walk through death itself, we're not walking alone. And when He is near, we can experience a deep peace and a grand perspective. I've found that when I'm in prayer, He reminds me of all the blessings He has already bestowed on me. He also gives me hope for what is to come.

4. Seek a renewed mind.

One of the areas where I believe women need God's help is seeking a renewed mind. Our minds are far too distracted with the meaningless and the urgent.

Jim Collins, a *New York Times* bestselling author, opens his book

Good to Great with the line, "Good is the enemy of great."[3] The good trap is precisely the snare that has gotten most of us. Our minds jump from one thought to another like a whack-a-mole, all while reaching a new state of fried. The constant barrage of stimulus drains the brain. Finally, we just throw up our hands in exhaustion and say, "It's good enough."

But good enough is not good enough. Our God is great, and our lives can experience this greatness if our minds are sanctified and renewed. We are called onward and upward. We are called to have victory over sin. We are called to become more holy. We are called to run the spiritual race set before us. "Good enough" is the endgame when we rely on our own strength. But "God enough" is the endgame when we lean on His strength and understanding. Instead of settling, we should redirect to the One who can give us the ability to be not only good enough but better still.

In Philippians 4:8, Paul wrote, "[Sisters], whatever is true…whatever is pure, whatever is lovely, whatever is commendable, if there is any excellence, if there is anything worthy of praise, think about these things." Our God knows that one of the enemy's favorite tactics is to feed us lies. The evil one schemes to get into your mind and push out the truth. The Devil can't alter God's wonderful plan for our lives, but he can make you *think* he can.

Todd Wagner, the senior pastor at Watermark, said it this way in a sermon: "Worry is thinking that God will get it wrong and depression is believing that He already did." Our God doesn't get it wrong, but our distracted minds often play tricks on us.

So what's a girl to do?

DRASTIC MEASURES

The enemy speaks untruth to stop us, drown us, take us out of the game, and ultimately make us distrust the heart and ways of God. We must fight daily to remain and think on truth, also known as the Word of

God. We don't need a knight in shining armor to rescue us—we need to learn how to swing the sword. Ladies, stop tiptoeing around your problems. Wield the sword and cut them off at the head.

If you want to make real progress, you can't simply rely on hope. Hope isn't a strategy. We need a good battle plan against the internal lies we face every day.

First, *you must empty.*

You must empty yourself of all the things that are feeding unwarranted anxiety, skewed perspective, and faulty thinking. You do this by putting guardrails on your mind and heart, by turning off the voices that speak lies. Anything that could lead you off the straight and narrow or divert your eyes away from Jesus should be on the chopping block.

This may mean you need to get off Netflix, turn off secular music, cancel the *People* magazine subscription, change BFFs, or take a break from social media. You may need to change your playground or your playmates. These things can easily lead to comparison, jealousy, lust, and a general numbing to sin. I used to justify listening to Top 40 music stations because I liked the beat. But I'm much more cautious now because the lyrics and messages behind many of our popular songs are corrosive to our souls.

Here's a simple rule of thumb—if you wouldn't let your teenager do it, then why would you? You may think this is drastic, but we are called "children of God" and need to think on things above. We protect our kids from things we know can distract their pure hearts, and we need to do the same to ourselves. Moreover, we need other godly women around us to help keep us accountable.

Second, *you must fill.*

We need to start filling our minds with the truth. If the first step was about removing the junk on the external front, the second step is replacing the vacancy with that which is true, just, honorable, pure, lovely, commendable, of moral excellence, and praiseworthy. The

God stuff. To know the character of God, we must meditate on His Word, listen to the Holy Spirit, and receive godly counsel from others. I've found that memorizing key verses combats anxiety and lies in moments of weakness. Consistently interacting with biblical teaching, Christian podcasts, a regular Bible study plan, and prayer time also helps to renew your mind.

Most importantly, spend time in the Word. Work to understand it. Wrestle with the text and seek out solid interpretations that allow you to experience God more intimately. It's not enough to know *about* God. You have to know Him personally and passionately.

If you are going to fight against some common lies that distract your mind and lead you into fear, then you need to be able to recognize the ugly ones, the pretty ones, and sugar-coated, deceptively palatable ones. Here are a few to get you started:

Lie #1: I'm not good enough, talented enough, or equipped enough.

When God calls you to obedience, you may be thinking He called the wrong person. Moses thought the same thing. When God spoke to Moses and asked him to lead the Israelite people out of Egypt, Moses' initial response was to question God's leadership choice. This may sound like a humble response on Moses' behalf, but it was actually a reflection of his lack of faith in God's sovereignty.

Moses' recognition of his inadequacy was a good thing. His lack of trust in God's ability to work through him wasn't.

When God calls you to love your spouse unconditionally, mother your kids with patience, sacrifice your time continuously, disciple others with love, serve the nations with kindness, and inspire others with your joy, you will never feel as if you can do it all. You will not feel as though you are enough.

Because you aren't.

Fortunately, your sufficiency and adequacy are not prerequisites for the job. When Moses questioned God's choice, God didn't respond by telling him, "But you are enough!" Instead, He reminded Moses of who He was. *I am enough.* He told him that He was the great I AM, the Creator of all mouths that talk, ears that hear, and eyes that see. His call and commission to Moses was about God's adequacy, supremacy, and sovereignty, not Moses' ability. Moses was simply the tool God chose for His purposes. And God wants the same for us.

If you don't feel good enough, talented enough, or equipped enough, remember that feelings aren't reliable. And realize the outcome is not dependent on you in the first place. Doubts and thoughts of inadequacy don't account for the sufficiency of our great God to accomplish His purpose for you. He will never ask you to do anything that His power and provision won't provide. And He will never ask you to go anywhere His presence won't comfort or guide you.

He calls. You go. He provides. I call it *surrendered effort*—surrender the outcome to God, but give your best effort in the process.

Girl, you aren't enough. Neither am I. But God is. Rest in that truth.

Lie #2: Maybe God won't come through.

Another lie that often weighs us down is the belief that God won't come through. He won't do what He says He is going to do. Maybe God isn't really listening. Maybe He doesn't really hear me. Maybe He doesn't really care.

I've stumbled over all these lies before, but when I anchor myself to the Word of God, I realize they all fly in the face of Scripture. First John 5:14-15 states, "This is the confidence that we have toward him, that if we ask anything according to his will he hears us. And if we know that he hears us in whatever we ask, we know that we have the requests that we have asked of him." And we're reminded in 1 Peter 3:12 that "the eyes of the Lord are on the righteous and his ears attentive to their prayer, but the face of the Lord is against those who do evil" (NIV).

When we step out in faith and do something risky, we want to know that God is really going to show up, guide us, empower us, and see us through it.

Elijah believed, and God showed up in a big way in 1 Kings 18. Elijah was so confident God would do exactly what He said He would do, he challenged the 850 prophets of Baal to an impossible contest. Both groups would set up an altar and a sacrifice to their gods, and whichever god answered by raining down fire from heaven would be considered the real God.

This was the ultimate leap of faith. Elijah was so sure the Lord was the only God that he was willing to bet his life on it in front of 850 pagan leaders and a crowd of half-hearted people. If God didn't light the bull and the altar on fire, then Elijah would surely be killed by satanic leaders.

But God did show up. After the leaders of Baal couldn't get their false gods to respond, the Lord responded in a mighty way. Not only did He bring down a fire, but He brought down a fire so fierce that it consumed the sacrifice, the wood, the stones, the soil, and the water around it. He consumed everything.

This is what our Lord does. When we ask according to His will and act according to His ways, God shows up and shows out. If He is willing to rain down fire from heaven for His people, can we trust Him to fight for our loved one with the chronic disease, the rebellious teenager with a hardened heart, or our unfaithful spouse?

I think you know the answer. He may not always present Himself at the time or in the way we expect Him to, but He always shows up. Our Lord hears our cries for help and delivers us.

He may deliver us *from* our troubles, allowing us to escape the problem or troubling circumstance. He may deliver us *through* our troubles, when His presence provides the strength and peace we need to endure. Or He may deliver us *by* our troubles. In these situations, our troubles may indeed lead us to death—and through our death we are delivered to Jesus, our ultimate victory, where all things will ultimately be made new.

Lie #3: My happiness is dependent on other things more than God.

Notice I said other things *more* than God, not *instead* of God. We Christians believe in God and think faith is important. But we also believe we need other things as well. We believe we need a good job. We believe we need a smaller jean size. We believe we need to get married or have a child. We believe we need one more dress, one more trip, or one more dollar. It's as if we think God is good, but not good enough.

God says to seek Him first *and then* all these things will be added to you (Matthew 6:33). He didn't say, "Seek the other things and then fit Me in."

We don't trust God enough. We don't think He'll come through and give us the joy and peace our hearts are longing for. We try to find satisfaction in our health, in athletic and intelligent children, in a nicer home, better job, more money, or a skinnier waistline. These things are more tangible, so we believe they are important. But God said the invisible things are what bring eternal satisfaction and significance.

When you begin to doubt that Christ is the only source of inner joy, reflect on these verses:

- "Those who listen to instruction will prosper; those who trust the Lord will be joyful" (Proverbs 16:20 NLT).

- "We fix our eyes not on what is seen, but what is unseen, since what is seen is temporary, but what is unseen is eternal" (2 Corinthians 4:18 NIV).

- "Whom have I in heaven but you? And there is nothing on earth that I desire besides you. My flesh and my heart may fail, but God is the strength of my heart and my portion forever" (Psalm 73:25-26).

- "He satisfies the longing soul, and the hungry soul he fills with good things" (Psalm 107:9).

- "You make known to me the path of life; in your presence there is fullness of joy; at your right hand are pleasures for-evermore" (Psalm 16:11).

FEAR FIGHTS FEAR

King Solomon was the richest and wisest man in the Bible. He had it all. He had hundreds of concubines on speed dial, the best chariots in the world, and a palace that would be highlighted on *Lifestyles of the Rich and Famous.* He had a house full of servants, and he built a temple to the Lord that was utterly magnificent. He ruled with style and intelligence. He's also penned the books of Proverbs and Ecclesiastics, which are filled with principles for successful living.

Before he died, he had something interesting to say about life. He said life is short. Don't spend your time living for all the stuff—the Gucci bags, the expensive dinners, the fancy degrees, the job promotions. They will die with you. Everything turns to dust. Enjoy life, but when all is said and done, only one thing matters: to fear God and obey His commands. If anyone would know, it would be Solomon. He had everything money could buy, and his ultimate conclusion was that stuff doesn't satisfy.

Isn't it interesting that the last words of this dying, experienced, and wise leader were to fear God? Not to enjoy Him, love Him, or draw near to Him. But to fear Him.

It is important to understand that the fear of God is not the same as the fear of failure or the fear of death. The Greek and Hebrew words for fear generally convey a positive message. The Hebrew word for fear is *yare*, which expresses the idea of reverence and respect. This fear acknowledges God's good intentions and makes a person receptive to wisdom and knowledge. In the New Testament Greek, the word is *phobos*, which means a reverential fear of God. In general, the fear of God is an attitude of respect, a response of reverence and wonder.

The fear of God is powerful and significant because it counteracts the fears we have in this world. We are anxious and distracted by many things on a daily basis, and these worldly fears often paralyze us. But the fear of God, the respect and acknowledgement that He fights for us in the eternal realm, can unchain us. He sets us free.

The fear of God fights the fears of this world. Fear fights fear.

This truth is so foundational that "fear not" is mentioned over 365 times in the Bible, one for every day of the year. This phrase carries eternal and significant benefits and is the antidote for a depressed and worried soul. The fear of the Lord is called "a fountain of life" (Proverbs 14:27) and "life itself, a full life" (Proverbs 19:23 MSG). It's given so that our "hope will not be cut off" (Proverbs 23:18 NIV).

The fear of God casts out the fear of this world. When we fear God in a healthy, life-giving way, we trust Him with the outcomes of life. This kind of trust isn't normal. It's an act of rebellion and bravery.

When I initiated my first unassisted Giant on the high bar, I experienced a brief moment of great fear. But I had the courage to go through it. I didn't want fear to keep me from experiencing the joy of living unashamed. I learned—and continue to learn—that the only way to land successfully is to take big swings and at the right time, let go.

You may be in that scary place right now. It may be with a personal relationship, your child's ADHD, an undiagnosed medical problem, or a growing reliance on a nightly drink. You have fears and anxieties.

You have worries and concerns. You have disappointments and failures. But our God has overcome all of these things. Sometimes you have to just go scared before you can go confidently.

I walked into our bedroom the other day and all three of my kids were laughing, smiling, and having the time of their lives. They were playing a game where they would jump off the bed and Jason would catch them. It seemed as though it was not too long ago that they were afraid to even step off the bed into the outstretched arms of one of us. Now they were giggling as they dove off the edge.

The difference between now and then? They knew their daddy would catch them. They could be fearless and joyful and excited about the unknown because they were confident Dad wouldn't drop them. They weren't sure *how* he would catch them, but undoubtedly, he would.

Your Daddy, our Father in heaven, will catch you. Go brave the fear.

6

Undivided Attention

I keep the LORD in mind always. Because He
is at my right hand, I will not be shaken.

PSALM 16:8 HCSB

heard it again. This time it was more pronounced. A loud, obnoxious noise was coming from the basement, and it was accompanied by hateful and hurtful words. At first I was hopeful my kids were just playing, but I was now certain this was not the case. They were fighting.

I didn't intentionally teach my kids how to have conflict, but I'm sure I've unwittingly modeled it a time or two. It's amazing how easy they've picked up on the skill of fighting and arguing, spewing damaging words that hurt another soul. I wish they picked up on cleaning that easily.

If I've noticed anything within parenting, it's that James 4 holds remarkably true:

> What causes quarrels and what causes fights among you? Is it not this, that your passions are at war within you? You desire and do not have, so you murder. You covet and cannot obtain, so you fight and quarrel (verses 1-2).

Arguments are caused by passions at war within us. We desire and do not have, so we fight. Or we desire and do not have, so we withdraw, get quiet, and hold grudges. Our passions can quickly gain mastery over our vulnerable flesh. And they often wreak havoc on our relationships.

In our house, we have four seasons of the year: winter, spring, summer, and college football. During the college football season, Allstate puts out a brilliant commercial with a character known as Mayhem. You know this guy. He's the human representation of disaster and chaos when he lights your house on fire, steals your car, and destroys your manicured yard. When Mayhem shows up, that's when Allstate steps in to save the day.

Passions are our Mayhem. When my children fight, I often want to helicopter in and handle the situation with force. It's easy to lash out on the one who is the most emotionally charged. It's lazy parenting, but it seems like the most natural thing to do.

But when I'm in the Word of God and anchored to Jesus, I see the situation differently. Instead of being frustrated and annoyed, I'm reminded that my children are just like all of us. Their passions are at war with their souls. They are torn between loving their sibling and hitting him with a Gatorade bottle, showing patience and showing them an upper cut. The little scuffles my kids get into are just a representation of how we can all be divided between being eternally minded and worldly minded.

Uncontrolled passions and untamed desires have an ugly grip on all of our hearts. When my kids fight, it's not a reflection of my failed parenting. It's a reflection of my kids' struggle with sin. When the desire to be right or win takes the sacred spot that only Jesus should occupy, they have developed an idol and are loving something else more than God. And that is the danger each of us face—having idols sit on Jesus' throne.

I've heard it said, "Show me your calendar and credit card statement and I will show you your idols." That's good. But I'd extend it to say, "Show me your arguments and conflicts and I will show you your idols."

What is the idol you struggle with most? Is it the desire to be right? To win? To defend? Is there a certain thing you want? Is it the need to be taken care of? Treated a certain way? Catered to? Is it jealousy? Maybe insecurity? Whatever it is, it will boil down to one of these three things: the lust of the flesh, the lust of the eyes, or the pride of life.

Regardless of your particular struggle, it's all slavery. It's all bondage to sin. I've been a slave to pride, desiring the applause of man. And I've been a slave to lust, insatiably desiring all the world has to offer. But those things have never satisfied. This place is not our home. We are aliens. We were made for eternity. Our souls were made for a heavenly kingdom. So any and all obedience to the flesh will leave our souls thirsting for more.

Charles Spurgeon once noted, "[If] Christ is not all to you he is nothing to you. He will never go into partnership as a part Savior of men. If he be something he must be everything, and if he be not everything he is nothing to you."[1]

I can get frustrated when my kids argue and fight. I can also get frustrated when I argue and fight. But both circumstances are just a reflection of the deep-rooted lies we continue to believe. Instead of meeting these situations with self-help nonsense or a show of force, we need to make these teachable moments opportunities to examine what has mastery over our hearts. These times may seem inconvenient, but they are unique moments when our hearts can be sanctified and we can begin to look more like Jesus.

Paul Tripp calls them "grace moments."[2] I like that.

If you are anything like me, your life has plenty of grace moments.

GRACE MOMENTS

I hate video games. And I especially hate Fortnite. The reason? Because my kids transform into thoughtless barbarians who bicker, fight, drool, and grunt when they play. We have all sorts of rules about screen time at our house, but I'm about ready to turn the Xbox into a piñata.

When my kids start playing these games, they are quick to display a disobedient and disrespectful attitude. It's like a mental drug for my boys. But I have to remind myself that these video games are morally neutral devices. The problem isn't the game—it's in the hearts of my children. The game just exposes the ugliness in their hearts.

It's easy to blame our sin problems on external things. When we remove those things and the issue still remains, the problem will manifest itself in new ways. The root cause will replant itself in other fertile grounds.

I never thought I'd say this, but I'm thankful for the grace moments Fortnite has provided. We've been able to have multiple conversations with our kids about battling performance-related significance, encouraging siblings, displaying patience, and understanding where rest and entertainment fit in our lives. These are all important issues they may face their whole lives, so addressing them early is a blessing.

In an effort to create "external boundaries" to combat the sin in our own hearts, we sometimes need to remove or limit the things that so easily entangle us (see Hebrews 12:1 and Mark 9:47). We need to create space to address the internal heart issues and nurture the soul-work. Since we all have blind spots, sometimes it's hard for us to see where an idol is filling the spot where Jesus and the Word of Truth should reside.

I had a grace moment with Reign a few weeks ago. I had told him he was not allowed to be on any sort of screen for a week. He knew the drill. It wasn't our first conversation around movies and games. So he nodded in agreement…and then snuck downstairs and started playing with the boys from his class at school.

I was not happy. Disobedience and deception are not allowed in our home.

When I inevitably caught him in the act, I asked him to turn it off. Immediately, I knew he was mad. He was caught in the place I often find myself—not being able to see past the temporary pleasure of the flesh. His selfish passions were ablaze.

After a long conversation, I began to understand the situation. He was worried about being left out when all his friends were playing. He wanted to be accepted and included, and on top of all that, he really liked playing Fortnite.

So we talked about it. Grace moments are rarely exciting conversations, but they are honest, heartfelt ones. I shared how disrespecting the authorities God places over us will eventually cause destructive patterns and big problems. We also talked about how we spend this precious resource called time. The more time we spend on mindless, addictive pleasures—not stewarding our time and talents for God's glory—the less satisfied and happy we become.

Our souls are meant to be mastered. The only question is whether they will be mastered by sin or mastered by righteousness, controlled by us or submitted to the Father. We are either walking down a path of life or one of destruction, but we are each going somewhere and following the influence of someone.

Reign needed to hear it. I needed to hear it again too. And so do you.

THE SOUL DIVIDED

Indulge me for a moment while I revisit the magnificent intricacies of the gospel. There are three Ps in the biblical story that unlock two Ps for you—peace and purpose.

As followers of Christ, we understand that Jesus died to pay for our sins, a debt we can never repay. We are delivered from the *penalty* of sin, and we accept Jesus' payment for our sins. In fancy theology speak, this is known as justification. While nothing externally may change right away, He alters our status in the heavenly realms immediately. Our sins are atoned for. He exchanges His righteousness for our unrighteousness and our standing before God is forever changed. This is the crazy good news.

The state of our souls is dependent on this gift and transaction. Jesus died for our sins. Every single one. And it wasn't just a historical event covering past sins. His death, and therefore His accompanying redemption, is at work in you now and for all eternity. It's a gift. This is G-R-A-C-E—God's Riches At Christ's Expense. It's the point of the entire biblical narrative.

But here's the problem: even though we have escaped the *penalty* of sin, we still experience the *power* of sin.

Even the great apostle Paul struggled with his changed soul operating in a fallen world. He said in Romans 7:15, "I do not understand what I do. For what I want to do I do not do, but what I hate I do" (NIV). This is not the idiotic mumbling of a drunken man, but rather the verbal acknowledgement that sin is powerful and our flesh is weak. He also said in Romans 6:12-14,

> Do not let sin reign in your mortal body, so that you obey its desires. And do not offer any parts of it to sin as weapons for unrighteousness. But as those who are alive from the dead, offer yourselves to God, and all the parts of yourselves to God as weapons for righteousness. For sin will not rule over you (CSB).

Sin doesn't rule us like it did before Jesus. Christ sent us the Holy Spirit to help us overcome the power of sin. When we trusted Jesus, we were justified, delivered from the *penalty* of sin. Now that the Holy Spirit is working in us, we are being sanctified, delivered from the *power* of sin. This regeneration is a constant refinement and inner renewal that strengthens the soul.

And someday—when our bodies die or when Jesus comes back— we will be delivered from the *presence* of sin. This is what we refer to as glorification. Imagine a world without sin. No more sadness, pain, or tears. No more loss, grief, or anxiety. No more hurt, anger, or confusion. Only Jesus. Only the complete satisfier, the ultimate life-giver. Games will be played without rebellion and relationships will be without jealousy, selfishness, and pretension. We will be able to enjoy all of the blessings of God without the urge to put them on His throne.

But for now, we are still divided and battling. We have these souls being constantly refined toward perfection, but we have these bodies that want to drag us down into death. We are like Lazarus—raised from death to life yet still walking out of the tomb in grave clothes. Our renewed, redeemed souls still have the desires of our flesh wrapped around them and we have to fight the agendas and motives of this present world.

We are delivered from the *penalty* of sin, but we still experience the *power* of sin. But one day we will no longer feel the *presence* of sin. If you understand this, then you can begin to find *peace* and *purpose* in Christ.

THE DOUBLE-MINDED MAN

I'm going to reiterate an important truth we discussed in chapter 2:

When God doesn't have your attention, He'll often disturb what does.

While this may not feel wonderful, it is actually a great mercy, because anything apart from Him will leave us empty and longing for more.

When my son confessed that he let the desire to be accepted by his friends and the temporary thrill of playing the video game trump the importance of obedience, I could relate. I'm a natural people pleaser, and I can wrestle with speaking the truth and hurting someone's feelings. It has me divided at times. Many of us fight this. It is the battle of a double-minded man.

As believers, we face this constantly. We want to trust Jesus with our souls, yet we tend to trust most of our control, peace, and satisfaction to things around us. We call it "balance" and we chalk it up as a good thing. But balance assumes two things are equally weighted. And in this life, nothing should get the same weight and priority as God.

James 1:6-8 says, "The doubter is like the surging sea, driven and tossed by the wind. That person should not expect to receive anything from the Lord, being double-minded and unstable in all his ways" (CSB). The doubter. She doesn't trust God completely. Her soul is divided. She wants "balance" in her life, but she is living in confusion. Our souls drown trying to serve two masters. We can't yield to the Spirit and to sin at the same time.

There is no balance in the kingdom of heaven. There are those with Christ and those against Him. There is no middle ground. Our situations will change, plans will be altered, and circumstances will challenge us, but Christ must be the solid ground on which we stand, the anchor that holds us in the midst of the storm.

You may not be practicing witchcraft or satanic worship, but not prioritizing your relationship with Christ is every bit as detrimental as those practices. Nothing is more powerful than a sold-out, single-minded, narrowly focused, kingdom-purposed saint who relies entirely on the power of Jesus.

THE DEVIL *IS* DISTRACTION

It's not that the Devil is good at distraction—the Devil *is* distraction. If you could hear him whispering to his fellow demons, it would sound something like this...

Keep them distracted.

Keep them running toward the mirages of life that look satisfying but hold no substance for their hungry souls. Keep feeding them cultural candy. Let them get high on the sugar rush of pursuing goals, marking off lists, and reaching for dreams. If you can keep them running toward

*accomplishments and plans that are always shifting, they won't have time
to stop and ponder the importance of life. Keep them busy.*

*One of our best strategies is allowing them to think they can have Jesus
and everything else. God and a consuming job. Jesus and the best vacations.
The Lord and an extramarital fling. Let them buy into the lie of "balance"
and that God doesn't want to get in the way of their personal pursuit of happiness. Let them believe they can and should have both. Both/and is a tactic that keeps their arms full, but either/or allows them to stop and think
about life. We can't have that. A hurried life is a dying life. Their constant
pursuit of perfection will make them weary.*

Keep them distracted.

*We do this by keeping them addicted. Technology can be a great asset to
you in this endeavor. If they are constantly getting pinged with notifications,
calendar events, emails, and texts, they will feel important even while their
souls are shriveling. The humans wreck themselves.*

Keep them distracted.

*Whatever you do, don't let them read the Bible. It is a formidable and
powerful weapon when used against us. When an exhausted soul opens the
Bible, she is quickly reminded that it is alive and active, applicable to everyone, full of wisdom, and a doorway to Christ. For whatever reason, it magnifies the Truth and that Truth is impossible to hide. If they do open the
pages, make it feel like a chore. Make it confusing. Make it dry. Whatever
you do, don't allow God to build a relationship through it. That is exactly
what He is trying to do.*

*Likewise, make them question the effectiveness of prayer. Even though
God always hears them, we need them to think He doesn't. Prayer needs to
feel elusive and cold. If they believe it's a one-way conversation, they will
quickly tire and revert to the old habit of leaning on their own strength.
God tries to meet them in the peace and stillness of prayer. We absolutely
can't allow this to happen. Even if we have to throw all of hell at them, we
have to stop the intimate gathering that the Father allows in prayer.*

Keep them distracted.

If you are wildly successful, your human will run and drive herself directly into the grave, never asking about eternal peace and purpose. But even if you are mildly successful, your human will one day wake up and realize she is old. She will wonder what happened to the years, to her life, to the opportunities. She will have wasted it all. And even if I can't take her soul, I will have taken her life.

Our mission will be accomplished. So keep them distracted.

NOT THE BOSS OF ME

Our daughter, Sage, is an amazing young lady with a strong personality. When she was little and learning to talk, one of the phrases she would blurt out when we tried to get her to eat vegetables or go to bed was "not the boss of me." It was cute at the time. But that won't be cute if she says it when she is 16 or 26. It will be a sign of a cold and defiant heart, one who thinks she knows best in all aspects of life.

Even though most of us don't utter the words "not the boss of me" in our daily lives, we often live them out through our actions. When we withhold forgiveness from a friend, our hearts are saying, "Not the boss of me." When we withhold sex and love from our spouse, our body is saying, "Not the boss of me." When we withhold compassion and care for the people around us, our mind is saying, "Not the boss of me."

Ironically, the things we try to control are often the things that end up controlling us. If you want to gauge what has a hold on your heart, see what happens when your "thing" is taken away. What bothers you when you don't get it? How do you feel when your smartphone is lost, when your boyfriend breaks up with you, when you don't get that exercise session in, or when you have to say no to that new purchase? How do you react when your son loses a football game, when you don't get the deserved promotion, when you can't afford a nice vacation, or when you don't get invited to ladies night? Do you crumble? Do you lose it? Do you become discontent, irritable, or angry?

Our culture has taken the sinful "not the boss of me" attitude and twisted it to make it sound righteous. They've tweaked it to make it sound empowering. It's the reason Ariana Grande sings about sex and female control in the song "God is a woman." It's the reason the feminist movement will shout that a woman can do whatever she wants with her own body, except if that female is a baby in utero. It's the reason women flaunt their bodies to grab the attention of the world. It's their way of shouting, "Not the boss of me!" But instead of being empowering, their actions quickly become demoralizing and destructive. They are not the boss, but rather are enslaved to the approval and applause of others.

In Luke 16:13, Jesus noted, "No servant can serve two masters." There are a couple of important parts to pay attention to in this verse. First of all, Jesus calls us "servants." This reminds us that we are designed to be willfully obedient to Christ and to surrender to Him. As an ex-athlete, I used to struggle with the idea of surrender. It sounded weak. But as God has continued to sanctify me, I've learned nothing is stronger than willfully, completely, and boldly serving our God. His call to obedience is a call to holiness, renewal, and regeneration. And I've never felt more fulfilled and empowered than when I'm serving our heavenly Father.

The second part of the verse reminds us that we can't serve "two masters." The first and best lie the Devil ever told was that "you will be like God" (Genesis 3:5). You can be human and like God at the same time. You can be both. You can have balance. You can go to church on Sunday and live like you want the rest of the week. You can watch that violent, degrading movie and listen to a *Desiring God* podcast. You can do both. You can have it all.

How's that working out for you?

The desire you have gnawing at your heart right now is the call to holiness. It's the desire to have endless joy and purpose. And it's the longing to have peace for your soul. No matter what you do in this life, it can only be satisfied in serving Christ alone.

When Jason and I first started dating, we were smitten with each other. We both went to great lengths to make the other happy. Instead of admitting there was a food or an adventure we didn't like, we would participate enthusiastically in nearly any recommended activity. A combination of young love and competitive firstborn attitudes kept us skipping and giggling through the early months.

I remember one particular winter evening when I wanted to go for a run. It was a balmy 30 degrees outside and snow covered a good part of the ground. I was an avid runner at the time and I was slim, fit, and had great endurance. Jason, on the other hand, was a muscular ex-college football player who had gone through four knee surgeries. I was built for distance, but he was built for speed. So you could imagine my surprise when he volunteered to go on a long run with me. I was skeptical, but I was giddy that he wanted to spend time with me. And I was a bit curious to see how this Clydesdale-like mammal was going to run like Secretariat.

As we laced up our running shoes and headed out, I remember taking it a bit easy for the first two or three miles. It was just a slow and steady jog. When we reached the halfway point, I recommended we pick up the pace. The look on Jason's face was priceless. It screamed, "I thought we already did!" But of course he wouldn't admit he was hurting. He just panted, "Okay" and continued breathing like a drowning water buffalo.

When we made it back to my place, I was feeling fantastic. But Jason looked exhausted and on the verge of collapse. Trying not to bruise his male ego, I suggested he relax and take a shower while I made dinner. He didn't argue in the least. He just crawled to the bathroom and eventually turned on the shower.

Fifteen minutes passed. Then 30. Then 60. At this point I was starting to worry. Did he pass out? Was the toilet clogged? Did he die?

Ten years and three children later, he finally admitted the truth about that night. When he got into the bathroom, he turned on the shower and laid comatose on the bathroom floor, desperately trying to recover. The running shower was hiding the fact he was moments away from cardiac arrest.

I loved that man then. And I still love him now.

I love him not because he nearly threw up trying to win my heart. I love him because he was willing to go through *anything* to be with me. And he has proved he would always do that over and over again. When I was bedridden during my pregnancies, he fed me, served me, and encouraged me. When I lost my grandfather and our first dog, he held my hand and let me cry. When I overloaded my plate with activities and then began to lose my mind, he gently smiled and helped me figure it out. I'm convinced Jason would do anything for me.

And yet, what he has done is nothing compared to what Christ endured for us on the cross. Our God became human, denied all the temporary comforts, and fought for our souls. He wasn't distracted by all the possibilities and luxuries He could have indulged in on earth. He was laser-focused on saving us and pointing our hearts to eternity.

It's hard to imagine that the God of the universe has undivided attention for each one of us. But He does. And He waits quietly and eagerly for us to avoid the daily distractions and find solitude in Him.

7

Heart Hammocks

In returning and rest you shall be saved; in
quietness and in trust shall be your strength.

ISAIAH 30:15

was raised in the middle of Kansas, infamously known as tornado alley. Naturally, as a young girl, I was fascinated with big storms, especially the ones that drew dark skies and brought a tornado or two. I grew up watching films like *The Wizard of Oz* and *Twister*. Truth be told, I might've even owned a pair of ruby red slippers and pretended my dog was Toto. We Kansans are awfully proud of our heritage.

I vividly remember clinging to my daddy on the front porch during a storm, eyes wide, hands shaking, and adrenaline pumping through my veins. Tornado sirens sang as we watched funnel clouds take shape in the distance. These massive storms had a way of making me feel small and vulnerable. But I was certain my daddy would protect me. I trusted his timing. I knew he wouldn't keep me out in the storm too long—just long enough to experience my own smallness and dependency. Just long enough to realize I had little control. Just long enough to understand that I needed him and his protection.

As my faith has matured, I've realized God is a lot like my daddy. Even in the most ferocious storms of life, He is comforting me and standing watch.

Because of my fascination with extreme weather, I've also studied hurricanes, which are an amazing and powerful phenomena. A category 5 hurricane has winds over 157 miles per hour, which is almost strong enough to mess up a 1980s poodle perm plastered with Aussie Hairspray. Yet deep in the middle of a hurricane, amid the swirling winds and crackling lightning, there is a strangely quiet center. This peaceful core, known as the eye, can be 20 to 30 miles of clear, sunny skies. People who have been in the eye of the storm are often shocked at the tranquility while just miles away, houses are being torn off their foundations and trees are being tossed around like toothpicks. But the area in the eye is completely calm, untouched and undisturbed.

So it should be with our souls. When unfaithful spouses and unforgiving bosses are swirling in our midst, our souls have to remain calm and steadfast. When both the car and the baby are pooped, our hearts should be at peace. We can't control what happens around us. We have to trust that Christ is on the throne of our lives and that things will turn out well, no matter how they turn out. But God stretches me in this. I don't have Carrie Underwood's faith—I don't often want Jesus to take the wheel. I want to hop in the driver's seat, white-knuckle it, and take the whole family for a ride.

The women I most admire are the ones who don't do this, who don't try to independently wrestle every problem to the ground. They are also the ones who are most at peace. Contrary to the current women's "you can do it all and have it all" agenda, they take a countercultural approach. They exemplify the promise of Exodus 14:14: "The LORD will fight for you; you need only to be still" (NIV).

Let's be very clear on something—"still" does not mean passive. "Still" doesn't mean a lack of obedience or effort. "Still" is not complacency. "Still" means extraordinarily faithful, trusting in the promises of God, waiting for the right time to act, seeking wisdom from other believers around us, and expressing our thoughts, feelings, and holy intuition in a way that lifts others up and glorifies Christ. The reason our hearts aren't at rest is because we try to do too much when there is only one thing necessary.

When I was learning to play piano, I was always rushing to the next note or chord. Every piece was allegro, whether it was designed for it or not. Finally my music teacher interrupted me and said, "Notes are just noise unless you recognize the rests in between them. Music is beautiful when we experience both the notes and the rests."

She was right. There is a certain tempo that all music—and our souls—must abide by. And the purposeful pauses are what allow us to differentiate between the beautiful sounds and activities. Sometimes the rest is short and sometimes it is long, but in every instance, it is necessary.

Everything in our world shouts "do." Everything in God's Word shouts "be." (The Bible also says "go" and "make" and "teach" and "obey," but these flow out of a soul that can *be*, and we will get to these later.)

I don't know what storm you are experiencing right now. You may have a prodigal child or an absent husband. You may be addicted to alcohol, shopping, gossip, or reality TV. You may constantly fight with insecurity, weight loss, faith, or your hair. Or you may not even know what is wrong but something feels awfully broken inside.

In the midst of the wildest storms and darkest clouds, we still have a Daddy protecting us and watching over us. So instead of panicking and running to all the temporary fixes the world offers, let's throw up a hammock in the middle of the storm and learn how to find rest for our souls.

BUSY AND HURRIED

If you are a woman in America today, you are going to be busy. Dinner has to get into little bellies, and bills have to be paid. Cars won't drive themselves (at least not yet), and clothes don't jump into drawers and onto hangers (but they totally should). Toys have to get put away, and emails have to get answered.

But we're not just busy. Our souls are hurried and our hearts are unsettled. And there's a monumental difference between the two. Busy is what we do with our bodies. Hurried is what happens to our souls. Busy is about getting to appointments and responsibilities. Hurried is when appointments and responsibilities get to us. We can survive in a busy world, but we won't thrive in the way God designed.

When we are hurried, we compensate by speeding everything along. We just want to get through it. Or past it. Or around it. Anxiety creeps in on us and we lack peace and contentment. We lose our patience with our spouses, and our kids feel more like a burden than a blessing.

Hurry can occur in two places: in our external life and in our inner soul. When our external life is hurried and our schedules are packed, we become physically exhausted. We run around to appointments, commitments, activities, and responsibilities, and when our heads finally hit the pillow at night, we are wide-eyed and unable to sleep.

When our souls are hurried, we feel overwhelmed. We are anxious when we look ahead and depressed when we look behind. I've spoken to thousands of women who feel this way. While it's comforting to know I'm not the only one who feels as though I should pop Prozac like Skittles, it's concerning to know we all feel as if we should.

Marsha is a single working mother who is trying to juggle three young kids, two jobs, and one mortgage. Half smiling, she said she only feels stressed out when she's breathing. Kim has been married for ten years, and from an outsider's perspective, she has it all together. But when she finally opened up, she wept and said her affluent house feels like a prison and her husband like a stranger who sleeps in the same bed.

Kaci is a well-known ministry leader at a megachurch. The more the ministry grows, the more trapped she feels. She is always praying and serving others, but she is the one who really needs comfort.

I get it. I'm a tightly wound, type A personality who constantly overcommits. My husband says I'm "time challenged" because I try to pack three hours of work into one hour and then I feel overwhelmed.

Yet I've learned that when I am overwhelmed, it's because I am focused on me. My "me" focus exposes my smallness. My weakness. My inadequacies in my circumstances. But when I turn to Jesus, when I see His greatness and His sufficiency, I am no longer overwhelmed at the situation; instead, I am overwhelmed by Him. And when I'm overwhelmed by Him—His sovereignty, His capacity, His grace, His love, and His protection—my soul finds rest.

Ironically, true rest can be found in the busiest of places. Mine was uncovered during a Spartan obstacle race.

If you're not familiar with a Spartan race, just imagine the pain of migraines, menstrual cramps, and mom jeans all at the same time. Then compound that pain by running uphill with rocks in your shoes. That's a Spartan race. It's basically just like a typical road race but off-road and with various obstacles that are placed strategically along the path. Those obstacles include scaling walls, pits of mud, and balancing beams. When I passed mile four, I was feeling tired but pretty good. Then I ran into the ninth obstacle, the bucket carry.

Carrying a bucket doesn't sound very intimidating at first. Unless it's full of sand. Larger around than your waist. Sitting at the bottom of a steep hill. That's when I realized I had a big problem. It made the mismatched socks in the laundry room seem insignificant.

I started by carrying the bucket in my arms. Then I put it on my shoulders. Then I swung it between my legs. Then I dragged it behind me. I tried everything possible and yet I was still only inching along. As I struggled, it struck me that I do the same with my daily life. I carry the burdens of the whole family in my arms. I put our health on my shoulders. I swing our happiness along. I drag unrealistic expectations behind me. And I wonder why I'm only inching forward.

Most of the time I just want Jesus to relieve me of my burdens. I want Him to tie a rope around the bucket and drag it up the hill for me. I want what Jesus can provide. But what I should desire is Jesus alone. He is the provision. He doesn't just pull our bucket up the hill. He ties the rope around our languishing bodies, places our buckets on His back, and leads us up the hill.

The reason we feel so hurried is because we believe it all depends on us. In reality, it all depends on Him. He bears the weight. He does the work. Our only responsibility is to live in unbroken dependence on Him.

In Matthew 6, Jesus reminds us, "Do not worry about tomorrow, for tomorrow will worry about itself. Each day has enough trouble of its own" (verse 34 NIV). Measured on its own merits, this verse has as much punch as a bag full of feathers. It's a cute saying on a nice Hallmark card, but it has no sustaining power. But when it is taken in context with the preceding verse—"Seek first his kingdom and his righteousness, and all these things will be given to you as well" (verse 33 NIV)—then it has supernatural strength.

While implementing healthy boundaries and creating margin for renewal and rest are helpful practices, life still happens and responsibilities are inevitable. It's not realistic to just check out (although at times it sounds rather tempting).

Is it possible to be busy and not hurried? I think so. We can run from swim meet to piano lessons to home-cooked meals without our hearts running on empty. We can handle the incoming text messages, sporadic family emergencies, and daily homework assignments without breaking a sweat. We just can't do it on our own.

The secret of a successfully busy life is learning to be joyful in all circumstances and anxious for nothing. In other words, it's a life constantly dependent on Jesus.

OUT OF CONTROL

Within four short years, I had four pregnancies, resulting in three C-sections and a miscarriage.

Shortly after, I began experiencing some strange symptoms in my weakened body. I ignored them at first because, as all weary and physically broken-down moms understand, our bodies go through the miraculously unimaginable to create life. One of my friends often says she is going to have T-shirts made for us that say, "I'm a superhero—I have the power to make humans."

I've always thought that hormones were part of the curse on women. I can't find the verse that supports it, but I'd argue there's a strong theological case to be made. Hormones just seem evil. They make you feel not normal. And that becomes the new normal. Which is abnormal.

Pregnancy permanently changes things—bigger feet, droopier boobs, lowered libido, patchy hair loss, and stretch marks in places that don't need premature aging. And that's just what happens on the outside. Postpartum anxiety, depression, and uncontrollable worry can also plague us, not to mention the guilt that can often settle in when we feel intimacy is off our radar and worry that our husbands may not understand. One more thing to fail at.

So there I was, overweight and sleep-deprived, with extra skin flapping in the wind. And my symptoms were getting worse. What started out as legitimate concern quickly morphed into unhealthy worry.

Because I have a medical background, I understood just enough of the possibilities surrounding my symptoms to make the situation scary. Numbness, pain, shaking, and unabated itching are not good signs. I tried to act as though it was all just in my head, but deep down, I began incessantly worrying.

I finally scheduled an appointment with my physician. Little did I know this was only the beginning. After a year of testing, months of lingering strep throat, a tonsillectomy, and neurological regression that included muscle twitching, dizziness, blackouts, difficulty swallowing, and essential tremors so debilitating I couldn't text on my phone, I was sent to the Mayo Clinic for a more intensive diagnosis.

I was fried. And completely exhausted. But what was even more incapacitating than the never-ending run around of doctors, testing, and waiting was what was happening to my soul. It was consumed with grief and fatigue. For the first time in my life, I was experiencing clinical anxiety.

The book of Matthew includes a story of the disciples being caught in a raging storm in the middle of the Sea of Galilee. They were frightened beyond compare even though Jesus was in the boat with them. I often wondered how they could lose their minds while the God of the universe sat next to them. Now I was doing the same thing. This was not just an occasional twinge of worry or a moderate amount of concern. I was falling apart. And even though I knew and trusted that God was with me, I was incapable of handing my fear over to Him.

I had convinced myself that I had the onset of ALS, otherwise known as Lou Gehrig's disease. And because there is no specific test to diagnose this illness, anxiety took over my life. It gripped my heart. It held me hostage. I couldn't breathe or function with any sort of joy. Every waking moment was consumed with fear. It was all I could think about.

And what consumes you, controls you. What fills your heart, rules your heart. It's the heaviest of all buckets to carry.

When things are going relatively well, our hearts are courageous. We are ready to do God's will, to accept whatever He has planned. But when the walls start closing in, our natural human reaction is to take control. How could God possibly have our best interest in mind when our child dies, when we lose our job, or when sickness overtakes us? And if we think He doesn't, then we decide we must step up and do it ourselves.

Tragedy unveils who or what we really trust. When I was healthy and life was going as planned, it was easy for me to trust Him. But when I realized I may not live long enough to watch my daughter walk down the aisle or to see my boys graduate, my trust in the Lord evaporated. My faith collapsed.

I failed. Just let it sink in. I had to. Failing isn't one of those accomplishments that gets you invited on the *Today* show or qualifies you for a TED Talk. But it is exactly what God needs to sanctify your heart and build trust in Him.

Many of us play this little game with God when it comes to completely trusting in His plan. I call it the "as long as" game. As long as God goes along with a bargain I find reasonable, I will follow and trust in Him.

As long as I don't have to tell my husband about my online shopping problem, I'll follow You.

As long as I can kiss my five-year-old good night and sing "You Are My Sunshine" for a few more years, I'll submit to Your plans.

As long as I don't have to be the only one standing up for gender norms at the school meeting, I'll speak up. Or at least write a strongly worded letter.

As long as I don't get slandered and skewered on social media, I'll point people to Jesus with my posts on Facebook and Instagram.

As long as I don't have to share my midnight bingeing on Oreos or my obsession with my waistline, I'll join a women's Bible study.

As long as I don't have to admit that I desperately need help parenting my kids, I'll continue my half-hearted bedtime prayers.

As long as I don't have to confront my husband about our complete lack of emotional and physical intimacy—and whatever issues that may come with it—then I'll continue striving to be a Proverbs 31 woman.

We don't really want to play the "as long as" game, but we do it because we desperately want to be in control. We use our obedience as a bargaining chip, as if God needs our faith to remain God. It's absurd, but people do crazy things when they feel an unmanageable burden on their shoulders.

It's amazing how tightly I start holding on to something when God reaches out for it and I'm not ready to give it up. I want life to be tidy and comfortable. I want to spark joy in everything I do. I want a schedule I can manage and control. I want to feel safe and protected. I want perfect.

God wants these things for me as well. But He doesn't need me as an advisor to make them happen. In fact, as a temporal being I'm highly unqualified to make eternal decisions.

When my health issues struck, I realized my knowledge of God was much more academic than experiential, and my life was merely seasoned with moments of redemption and peace. I had stood in the pews and sung about how long, how wide, how deep, and how high God's love was for me, but I had never leapt into the unknown, trusting that this same boundaryless love would catch me. I placed my hope and pursuit of joy and purpose in the things that were out of my control and not in the One who holds it all together.

I felt out of control, but in reality, it was just out of *my* control. God was still on the throne and everything was playing out according to His masterful plan. He was beginning to show me that situations are never in my control, but how I react to them are.

In the book of Daniel, there is an amazing story of three faithful Jews named Shadrach, Meshach, and Abednego. They are shining examples of recklessly trusting in God despite debilitating circumstances. As exiles in the pagan, materialistic Babylonian culture, they lived under the control of the evil king Nebuchadnezzar. He required all the people to bow down to an enormous statue erected to honor himself. Those who refused would die by fire.

These three men did not waver or budge. They didn't convene a Bible study to decide what to do. They didn't phone a friend. They didn't consult with the masses online. They immediately responded by highlighting the sovereignty of the one true God, Yahweh, and their allegiance to Him. They would not bend a knee to any earthly king and were willing to be thrown into the flames if necessary.

This infuriated King Nebuchadnezzar, and he ordered that the furnace be heated to seven times its normal heat to completely incinerate these obstinate peasants.

It's hard for me to relate to Shadrach, Meshach, and Abednego and their situation. They got up one morning thinking they'd put in a full day's work, but after an unpredictable series of events and a confrontation with an arrogant dictator, they were now bound in ropes and prepared to have their skin melted off. That doesn't resonate with me. I don't know how I'm supposed to prepare my heart for this type of thing. When I'm comfortably sipping my tall flat white (with two stevia) at the local Starbucks, and the woman next to me asks why I'm reading the Bible, will I hesitate to share the hope of Jesus? Will I fear the awkwardness of sharing with a stranger in a public place? Or when I hear two arrogant radio hosts boasting about the joys of sexual promiscuity on the air, will I call in and share God's plan for marriage in front of millions of listeners?

I fear that I care too much about what people think of me. And that's the point—these three faithful men did *not* care about their lives. They cared more about their God and trusted His plan. They were prepared for whatever came their way. They trusted God with everything—and we often struggle to trust Him with anything.

There's no scripture that specifically states that if you defend God, you won't be burned at the stake. There's also no scripture that promises God will step in and save you from ignorant or arrogant dictators, bosses, husbands, or hair stylists. Swimming against the forceful current of this postmodern culture and its antibiblical agenda requires faith and an eternal perspective. And most importantly, a heart that pursues and longs for God more than anything else. No fire could put out that flame. It carries an unshakable purpose, with an overwhelming peace that results in a supernatural willingness to sacrifice and step out in unfathomable ways.

If you remember the story, God was exceptionally patient in His response, probably to the discomfort of Shadrach, Meshach, and Abednego. They were bound with ropes, forcefully handled by guards, and tossed into the fire. But they didn't burn.

To the amazement of Nebuchadnezzar and everyone watching, the three faithful Jews were walking around in the fire, untouched and unharmed. And there was a fourth form in the fire with them. We don't know if it was an angel or the preincarnate Jesus Himself, but we know for certain that the divine interceded. The text actually says that the person in the furnace with Shadrach, Meshach, and Abednego looked like a son of the gods. But what's interesting about the story is that God didn't deliver the men from the fire. He delivered them in the fire and through the fire.

God can certainly step in and deliver us from a failing relationship or a collapsing dream, but it seems to be His least preferred strategy. We rarely learn genuine and trusting faith when we are bailed out. In most instances, He works in and through our circumstances, refining and sanctifying us as we walk in faith, step-by-step. Going through the fire stretches and strengthens us, even though it can be uncomfortable at the time.

When we are in the fire, we see Him for who He really is. Faithful. Dependable. Lover of our soul. The good, good Father. The One who is able. The Alpha and the Omega. The One who spins planets and breathes life into our souls. The Savior who cares for us more than anything and was willing to be ripped apart, broken, scourged, and crucified on the cross for our sins.

He is the true satisfier and the ultimate object of our worship.

I want to be more like Shadrach, Meshach, and Abednego. I want that type of faith. I want the kind of intimacy with God that allows my soul to rest untouched by the fires that surround me. I want it on a daily basis when the kids flush enough toilet paper to plug the Hoover Dam and when the washer starts acting like a sprinkler. More importantly, I need it when close friends go through a divorce, I'm worried sick about my personal health, or I'm grieving the debilitation loss of a cherished loved one.

Intellectually, I know I'm not supposed to worry. But the possibility that I could have a dismal, life-threatening disease had me very worried and I became obsessed with it. My worry was a result of distrust in God's goodness. Thankfully, the experts at Mayo were able to diagnose my illness. They called it dysautonomia.

Dysautonomia is a dysfunction of the autonomic nervous system, the system that regulates our breathing, heart rate, blood pressure, and temperature. And mine is chugging along like a dryer full of army boots. Doctors are still trying to figure out the condition. They don't know what causes it or if it will progress to something worse. They do know, however, there is no cure.

I still experience pain, twitching, and tremors on a daily basis. The symptoms didn't miraculously go away. But God did start working on my soul and allowed me to see more clearly the purpose of my life. He showed me that even when the situation is unpredictable, I can find a place of peace in Him. Even when the fire rages on the outside, I can find rest on the inside when I gaze upward. This confidence doesn't come because we are delivered from the situation—I'm still living with dysautonomia every day—but because we have faith in the Creator of all situations and believe He is ultimately good.

I thought peace was something I had to manufacture on my own. I thought my purpose was something I had to figure out along the way. Maybe if I took enough Enneagram, spiritual gifting, and personality tests I would find the answer. Turns out that peace isn't a state of mind or a destination. Turns out purpose isn't something you magically become enlightened to or discover. It doesn't come with perfection in the form of a perfectly controlled life. It's a person. And it is found in Jesus Christ, the perfect One.

My hands still shake but my heart doesn't. I have days when the physical symptoms are debilitating, but I'm learning that things out of my control are not out of His control. In John 16:33, Jesus said, "I have told you these things, so that in me you may have peace. In this world you will have trouble. But take heart! I have overcome the world" (NIV).

It's comforting to know that we can have true, deep, internal peace and that we can take heart because of who was meant to fill it: Jesus. We can't orchestrate peace on our own by losing weight, washing our face, scheduling a mani-pedi, or buying new shoes. It is through Christ alone.

And that is good news.

SACRED SPACES

Empty spaces are sacred spaces.

Books have margins and roads have shoulders for the same reason. We need space—places that aren't constantly bustling with activity. The same can be said about our souls. In our technology- and activity-obsessed lives, it is vital that we intentionally create empty space.

> My hands still shake but my heart doesn't.

We rarely have quiet moments in our life. I'm not talking about time to sleep or planned vacations or those moments when you lock yourself in the closet to escape the inmates who share your last name. While those times are important, most moments are masquerading as sacred space. I'm talking about real quiet moments that create space for our souls.

In these moments, we shouldn't attempt to accomplish anything. Or make progress. Or organize our schedules. Our goal should be to create enough space so that the Holy Spirit and the Word of God can infiltrate our lives. These are the times we disconnect from our Fitbits, our smartphones, and Netflix. These are the moments we put down our books and our emails. These are the moments we lay aside our agendas and to-do lists.

And do nothing.

Does that thought make you smile or squirm? While it makes most people smile, the truth is, we are all like dogs chasing a car. We wouldn't know what to do with *nothing* if we caught it.

I was standing in my kitchen the other day, feeling utterly discouraged, restless and frustrated with certain people in my life. Being a recovering people pleaser, I was wrestling with the thought that someone may be upset with me. I felt hurt and misunderstood.

Instead of grabbing the Bible sitting on the island, I instinctively reached for my phone to scroll through Facebook and Instagram, unconsciously hoping some clever pictures and funny stories would distract me. And it worked. For a few minutes, I didn't feel anything.

Therein lies my problem. And yours. We are distracted and numbed by the constant noise in our lives. The noise numbs us from the pain and hurt others have caused us, the abuse we have endured, and the feelings of unworthiness and unacceptance. It distracts us from our inadequacies and even our boredom. The problem is that the noise is like a warm blanket. It's comforting. So we quickly wrap ourselves up in it. It fills our space; but it doesn't fulfill us. Distraction is only a temporary drug. It wears off quickly. And then we have to go back for another hit.

Some of us suffer from an abusive past. Some of us struggle with food addiction. Some of us find comfort in gossiping. Some of us are obsessed with how we look in the mirror. Some of us feel trapped in a relationship. Some of us feel we are inadequate parents. Regardless of what your personal struggle may be, it is far easier to ignore it or tuck it away so you (and others) don't have to deal with it.

These things control our minds, consume our thoughts, and therefore capture our hearts.

The reason we are spent is because it is exhausting carrying these burdens around everywhere we go. When we have some sacred space, instead of anesthetizing ourselves with the latest celebrity news article or the online deal at Gap, we need to bring it into the light with Jesus. God never intended for us to fix ourselves. He said He would take care of it Himself when we come to Him, when we focus our attention and affections upon Him.

Empty space is sacred space. And sacred space is sanctified space when Jesus is invited in. We need sacred space where we can abide with Jesus.

Which begs the question, how do we create sacred space consistently? To put it into practice, I've simplified it to:

Devote daily. Withdraw weekly. Measure monthly. Abandon annually.

Devote daily (30 min–1 hour).

The Bible records Jesus praying 25 different times during His earthly ministry. On multiple occasions, Jesus purposely distanced Himself from other people so that He could commune with His heavenly Father. He spent time alone with God in the wilderness (Matthew 4:1-11), up on the mountaintop after feeding the 5,000 (Matthew 14:23), and early in the morning while it was still dark (Mark 1:35). Jesus knew the importance of sacred space and time.

Devote a portion of every day to be in God's Word. Don't do it because you feel a religious obligation or because you need to accomplish a spiritual task, but do it to spend time with the God who loves you. Whether it is short or long prayers, deep theological studies, or brief Scripture readings, take time daily to share your heart and confess your struggles with the Lord.

If you are too busy to spend time with God, you are too busy. Everybody makes time to eat and sleep daily. Time with the Lord is even more important than that, since He created both the food you consume and the air you breathe. When you create sacred space by devoting daily, you establish the healthy spiritual habit of looking to God and relying on His strength. It also creates a sanctuary of silence in a day normally clamoring with noise.

Withdraw weekly (2–4 hours).

The Sabbath has always been a sacred time for believers, not because any particular day of the week is special, but because it reminds us to refocus our attention on the Creator. And because when God created the earth, He worked for six days and then took the seventh day to intentionally rest.

Many of us have lost the discipline of withdrawing weekly. It doesn't have to be an entire day, but we do need planned times to get away and unplug from our daily routines and responsibilities. Sometimes my sweet beloved, Jason, will give me an hour or two on a Saturday or Sunday afternoon to grab a Starbucks, pray, and spend some time in silence or in the Word.

Withdrawing weekly will look different for different people. A wise Jewish proverb suggests that if you work with your hands, take a sabbath with your mind. If you work with your mind, take a sabbath with your body. In other words, if you are a busy mom who is regularly Ubering your kids around town, reassembling the dirty car seats, bathing the overtired tornado toddler, and cleaning kitchen floors that have been recklessly painted with glitter slime and spilled dog food, you probably won't be refueled training for a marathon. Go listen to a podcast that will challenge rigid assumptions and long-held, preconceived ideas. Read a book that will stretch your mind. On the other hand, if you sit at a computer all day, take half a day to go for a long walk, garden, or wrestle with your kids.

Measure monthly (4–8 hours).

We can't improve on things we can't measure. There is real wisdom on taking a step back at least once a month and reflecting on our lives, purpose, and relationship with God.

We often make the mistake of trying to measure our internal growth with an external list of accomplishments. This leads to frustration and fatigue. Instead, we should think of our spiritual growth like an umbrella. An umbrella doesn't change the weather, but it does change our experience in the weather. If life is raining family emergencies, the spiritually wise woman will walk through it under God's provision. God may not change our circumstances, but He will refine us and transform how we react in those circumstances.

There is no substitute for digging into Scripture, spending time in prayer, and seeking honest feedback from other women. These three aspects are critical to spiritual growth. If you are not incorporating these into your life, then you need to start here. I often have women stop me and say it is difficult to find time for all of this. It can be, but I encourage all of us to take back our daily moments. If you are folding laundry, you can listen to the Bible on audio. When you are standing in the grocery store line, you can be praying for your family. While you are waiting in the carpool line, you can have an intentional phone call with a friend. None of these actions dramatically change our daily routine, but they can catalyze exponential growth in our souls.

Then spend time once a month reflecting on your growth and what the Lord is doing in your life. Pull out that dusty journal and make a list to reflect on and recount the lessons learned and God's faithfulness and provision. Meet with your mentor or trusted group of friends, those walking alongside you, and *count the fruit*. As the Old Testament prophets would often construct an altar to commemorate important redemptive moments, these intentional pauses of reflection will be your "stones of remembrance." We are looking for progress, not perfection. No gold stars or trophies are going to be handed out. We want to make intentional, iterative changes so that we learn to walk more closely to our Savior.

Abandon annually (3–7 days).

Busy has become a badge of honor in our society. The standard answer to the question "How are you doing?" is "Good, but busy." Somehow we have convinced one another that being active equates to being on task and productive.

I see people in the gym spending hours of their day lifting weights and spinning tirelessly on a bicycle with little to no progress in their physical condition. They are committed, often overcommitted, but to the wrong movements, in the wrong progressions, and not in focused, beneficial ways. Sadly, many of us adults are operating in the same way, adding unnecessary events and items to our lives.

As a counterweight to calendar madness, we need to abandon our schedules annually, or unplug for about a week every year to spend undistracted time with Jesus. While the goal of abandoning annually is not to empower you, you will feel empowered. It does not give you more independence, but you will gain freedom. It is not to encourage you, but you will be greatly encouraged. Because when you focus on the Savior and spend time with Him, all the other rewards will come. They are an outflow of a life that finds purpose and peace in pursuit of Him.

Abandoning annually is not a vacation, at least not the way we typically experience vacation. Sacred space is not leisure. In his book *The Rest of God*, Mark Buchanan states that "leisure has become despotic in our age, enslaving us and exhausting us, demanding from us more than it gives."[1] We often come back more exhausted from the trip to the mountain or beach than when we left.

Abandoning annually should have the opposite effect. Creating a week of sacred space should fulfill and sanctify us. The root of the Hebrew word for sanctify literally means "to betroth." To pledge marriage. To choose to commit yourself, all of yourself, to this man or this woman, and then to honor that commitment. Sanctifying time works the same way. You are to commit yourself to Jesus for the entire time.

Leisure might initiate guilt, but sabbath never does. Sanctified, sacred, intentional time begets attention. And attention to our hearts, purpose, and identity, through our time with our Lord, is exactly what we need.

Jesus went off in the morning to find space and quiet time to pray.

That place for you may be a plane ride away or a long weekend locked up in a hotel room a mile away. Ask a spouse, friend, grandparent, or trusted sitter to watch your kids. Exchange the favor. Do whatever it takes. Fight for the time to be alone with God.

Pursue Him during this time. It should look like an extended version of your daily appointments with God.

How do you do this? Take your Bible, a journal, and a pen. Turn off your phone or set it aside. Start with prayer, asking the Holy Spirit to open your eyes to the surpassing worth of Christ through the knowledge of His Word. Ask Him to awaken you to insight that would convict, direct, encourage, and enable you to see God as supremely valuable.

Then dig into the Word of God. He will meet you, speak to you, and fulfill you. His Spirit will allow you to pray through the words of Scripture. Pray them out loud. Meditate and think deeply on the words as you read them slowly to your heart. And wait for Him to move inside of you.

If you are feeling consistently spent, then devoting daily, withdrawing weekly, measuring monthly, and abandoning annually will help you tremendously. There is much more to be said about each of these disciplines, but instead of trying to cram them all into one chapter like toys stuffed into my purse, I wanted to plant the seed and continue to water it throughout the rest of this book. For now, think and pray about how you can create more sacred space in your life.

I AM, YOU BE

In John 15:4-5, Jesus told His followers,

> Abide in me, and I in you. As the branch cannot bear fruit by itself, unless it abides in a vine, neither can you, unless you abide in me. I am the vine; you are the branches. Whoever

abides in me and I in him, he it is that bears much fruit, for apart from me, you can *do* nothing (emphasis added).

I imagine that as Jesus was walking along the path with His disciples, He encountered a vine that was bearing fruit. He made a salient analogy to help them grasp the idea that to find their purpose and experience abundant joy (John 15:11), they would need to *be* attached to the vine before they *did* anything else.

We want to *do* something. He is calling us to *be*.

The God of the universe refers to Himself as Yahweh, the great "I AM." If we are to be like Him and with Him, it is not surprising that He is asking us to just be. After all, He did name us human beings and not human doings.

We often think God's will for our lives involves an expectation to do something, when in fact, He simply wants to be with us. He wants to be the object of our worship and the satisfier of our souls. When we abide with Him and in His Word, we will be at peace. We will be at rest. We will be still. We will be free of worry. And this is what will ultimately translate to a life of active obedience and fruitful effort. The do is an outworking, an effect of being centered and purposed in Him, loving Him, and pursuing Him above all. He is the better portion that Mary had found. Obedience, mission, and calling are not our purpose. As Tozer said, our purpose is "that we might worship God and enjoy Him forever."[2] This God-glorifying, Christ-exalting mission will meet every desire we have, fill every craving, and satisfy any longing in our soul. The inevitable effect is a life fully surrendered, obedient, and not searching for significance in other lesser things. We must love God first.

It doesn't matter if you are a doctor, lawyer, fitness instructor, barista, or stay-at-home mom. It also doesn't matter whether you are feeling strong, sad, hopeful, anxious, excited, depressed, or exhausted. God is ready to meet you where you are, no strings attached.

And there you'll find the Perfect you've been chasing all along.

8

Meant to Be

You are a chosen race, a royal priesthood, a holy
nation, a people for his own possession, that you
may proclaim the excellencies of him who called
you out of darkness into his marvelous light.

1 PETER 2:9

hen I was 13 years old, I reentered society. I went from being homeschooled back to public school. I loved being a homeschool kid, but when I stopped training and competing as a gymnast, my parents said I should go back to a *normal* school with *normal* people and I was excited. As I sat in a class of nervous, chatty girls and acne-ridden, awkward boys, I prepared myself for a *Saved by the Bell* experience.

Because gymnastics had demanded so much of my time, I hadn't participated in any other sports. So when middle school volleyball tryouts came around, I mustered the courage to give it a shot. With a mouth full of braces and a rock-solid, aerosol-sprayed ponytail, I strutted confidently out onto the court.

I desperately wanted to make that team. I mean *desperately*. I wanted it more than I wanted to kiss Brad Pitt. All the cool girls played volley-ball, and I wanted in the coveted circle of ponytails and glitter. I'd be okay if I made the second team—since I barely knew the rules of the game—but I had to make the team.

When the day of reckoning came, I crowded around the door with at least a hundred other nervous and anxious girls. Before email and newsfeeds, all of our information was tacked to the school door, like Martin Luther's 95 Theses. All of us teenagers believed our destiny hung in the balance.

As soon as all the giggly girls cleared out, I slowly made my way to the front. I felt a lump forming in the back of my throat—a lump I've grown all too familiar with over the years. It starts like a small knot, but then it quickly hardens and makes me feel as though I'm going to suffo-cate. I quickly scanned the first team list…nothing. And then my eyes scrolled farther down to the second team…nothing.

Reality set in. They didn't want me.

THEY DON'T WANT ME

We often say the three most powerful words in the English language are "I love you." I don't believe that is the case. I think the three most powerful words are "I choose you."

For the first time in my adolescent life, I felt the sting of being left out. So I did what any normal middle school girl would do. I cried.

I'm an ugly crier. Some women weep softly into a Kleenex, but not me. I don't just shed a few tears. Oh no. I break down and sob while snot runs down my face and my eyes swell up like I'm having an aller-gic reaction. I look like Elmer Fudd. It's not pretty.

Being unwanted forced me to wrestle with my identity. *Who exactly am I? Does it matter if they don't want me? Where do I belong? Should I care what people think and if I have their approval?*

Even as a grown woman, I still wrestle with these questions from time to time when I'm not relying on the Truth. The volleyball tryout didn't scar me, but it opened my spiritual eyes to see things I hadn't seen before. I thought I was leaning on the Lord, but in reality, I was just leaning on my own strength and capabilities. My emotional breakdown was evidence of this. I was relying on me.

My feelings often tell me I'm vulnerable and out-of-control. I don't like it. But the reality is that God is always in control of my life, He wants what is best for me, and He sacrificed His own Son as proof. I often forget this, especially when my feelings and emotions take over.

As women, our feelings and emotions can be one of our greatest assets *or* one of our greatest liabilities. When they are kept in their proper place—submissive to the Word of God—they allow us to be compassionate, insightful, accepting, and connected to the souls around us. But when our feelings take over and replace God, we can be swayed by gossip, worried by circumstances, tempted by lies, and anxious for everything.

Where we find our identity is exceptionally important. We'll either find it in Christ, or we'll spend our whole lives trying to find it in something else, which will never satisfy. Even as a believer, you may know Jesus as Savior, but do you know Him as your *Completer*?

God is still working on me, and He is still working on you as well. Every day I struggle with acceptance, "trying out" with those around me, inside my house, outside my circle, and on social media. I've learned that I struggle as a people pleaser and approval seeker. Even as I write this book, I'm fighting the sneaky voice inside my head that's saying, *What if these words don't resonate with anyone? What if God won't use you? What if you are a complete failure?*

What if you don't make the team?

Every day I long to be accepted by *you*. It's irony's biggest performance, but I desperately want to be accepted by the women with whom I want to share Jesus.

I want to be liked by my friends at church and the mom who lives next door. I find unhealthy satisfaction in hearing that I'm "the neighbor who is just such a joy."

I want to be invited to all the ladies events and kids' parties, even though I'm an introvert and I don't really want to go! But I want to be invited and I want my kids to be included and accepted so that we feel as if we belong.

I want my husband to think I'm amazing. I want him think I'm pretty good at this wife thing and that I'm pretty. I want him to adore me despite my ugly habits and non-supermodel body (this baby pooch isn't going anywhere no matter how many sit-ups I do).

I want my kids to think I'm wise and fun and interesting. I want to be that mom who can chat for hours about NFL draft picks, Squishy collections, and the hottest fashion trend. I could easily find identity in being the "cool mom."

But deep down, I want to know God more. I want to please Him. I want to be obedient and holy. Even though I'm failing on an hourly basis, I want to run into His arms for a hug, because I know I'm always accepted and comforted there.

This fight for acceptance, belonging, and approval is hard. And continuous. But I'm learning to struggle well. And you can too.

THE APPROVAL TRAP

When I was young, I wanted to make my parents proud. I ran on affirmation like a car does on gas, seeking praise and approval with accolades in school, sports, and even good moral behavior.

My whole world revolved around my accomplishments. I wanted to be first, on top, number one. I believed that's what others expected of me, and therefore, it was what I expected of myself. What I didn't realize was that I was slowly drowning under the unnatural weight of self-induced, performance-based acceptance and the endless chase for perfection. God wasn't my greatest delight. I found approval in what I could do and what others thought of me.

As God matured my heart, I learned I loved other's *conditional* affirmation more than I loved God's *unconditional* acceptance. In other words, I liked how others made me feel more than I liked the fact that Christ accepted me, regardless of my performance.

Fortunately, God knew many of us would struggle with this. So He had Paul pen, "I'm not trying to win the approval of people, but of God. If pleasing people were my goal, I would not be Christ's servant" (Galatians 1:10 NLT).

From my experience, most godly women trust Christ with their salvation—just not their daily lives. We often seek release and rest in places that can't provide it and then wonder why we thirst for acceptance.

Sisters, we are accepted in and through Christ alone. His acceptance allows for peace in conflicts. We can take the target off of other people, because we know the real enemy. We can become less defensive, trusting He will right all wrongs. His acceptance allows us to lower walls in a fight, apologize first, and freely forgive.

His acceptance trades yelling for praying. It confronts and condemns sin, demolishes strongholds, and allows us to die to our flesh. It allows us to encourage others, not to wallow in our own insecurities. It allows us to stand when we need to rise and sit when we need to back down. It keeps us quiet when we feel like shouting and vocal when we're scared to talk.

His acceptance quiets our hearts. It keeps us from being consumed by the awkward glance or snarky word. It stops us from worrying about what others think. It quiets our minds. We don't have to replay the conversation that didn't go right or end smoothly. His acceptance allows us to play the role we were designed for, ambassadors of His perfection and grace.

When we don't find our approval in Him, we aren't the only ones hurt. Others are hurt as well. Those who don't understand their personal identity in Christ and embrace His unconditional acceptance lack the ability to encourage others. And this is a big, big problem.

God designed exhortation and encouragement as a gift of the Holy Spirit to equip and sustain us. If we stop cheering for each other, speaking life-giving words, and going out of our way to be outspoken on things that matter, we deflate the body of Christ. The word *encourage* literally means "to inspire with courage," and we are being disobedient when we don't affirm and don't give heart and hope to one another through the trials of life.

Too often I have seen encouragement and praise withheld for fear of causing someone to become prideful. I've also seen them withheld because the giver doesn't want to appear small. Conversely, I have seen affirmation in the form of disingenuous flattery used for manipulation or to selfishly win the affections of the other person. Neither are what God had in mind. But both stem from an immature heart that seeks approval from those around her.

Fruitful encouragement always speaks with honesty, seeks the other person's best interest, removes jealousy, and lavishly praises spiritual growth, faithfulness, and dependent effort. We should not only give praise freely in these areas, but intentionally look for opportunities to uplift and love others in this way.

Sisters, we are already accepted. So let's pray big prayers, extend crazy amounts of grace, and lavish God-glorifying praise on one another. It won't empty you. It will fill you.

FULLY KNOWN

I used to believe that once I made it through the gauntlet of middle and high school, I would no longer struggle to belong. Or perhaps I just wouldn't care anymore. But as I've entered my forties, I've found this isn't true. The desire to be invited, to feel part of a group and have genuine friends, never goes away.

Now it just looks different. On social media, we see pictures of our friends having a great time on a girls night. We overhear the woman in the checkout line chatting about the trip she took to the spa with her "tribe." We find out we've been left off the group text with all the other ladies at work. And the same middle school feeling comes back—we long to belong.

Of course, it would be easier to be included if we weren't so stinkin' busy. We had to take the dog to the vet for the third time this week, the baby is running a temperature, work emails are piling up, and the conflict with the hubby still isn't resolved, even after the three-hour talk and makeup sex.

We rarely have time for deep relationships. And when we do, we're scared of getting close. Insecurities still plague us. We wrestle with awkwardness. We worry about being interesting. What if the way we dress, the places we eat, or the kids activities aren't acceptable? What if we aren't cool enough, popular enough, or rich enough?

But here's the catch. Even if you were invited to every gathering, included in every group text, and desired by every male, would you be joyful and content?

Absolutely not. Because people and attention can't fill a space designed only for God.

God wired us and designed us to first live in relationship with Him. And once that is established and solidified, then we can live peacefully in community with genuine friends who love us despite our faults and sins. But He never intended for us to define our worth and value through these relationships with other people. They can never fill our joy tank.

When we run around searching for significance and identity in all sorts of things with all sorts of people, it's like frantically searching for your sunglasses...even though they are on your head. You can't go find something you already have. Contentment and peace are right there in front of you. With Jesus.

Our souls get exhausted if they have to constantly fight for acceptance and approval. But in Christ, we don't have to. As Paul reminds us in Philippians 4:19, "God will supply every need of yours according to his riches in glory in Christ Jesus." Every need—including your desire to belong.

But maybe you are not one of those women who struggles with belonging anymore. Maybe you're settled in your relationship and identity with Christ. Maybe you already have a strong group of close friends. If so, God has something for you to do.

Break the circle. Invite others in. Look for the outsider. Make room for others.

Wherever you go, look for the introvert, the new mom, the tired soul, or the obnoxious parent. Look for the neighbor of a different race, the parent with a special needs child, or the family that just moved to town. They may be sitting quietly, yelling from the bleachers, or acting as though they are doing something important on their phones. They're not. They are desperately waiting for you to interrupt, for you to invite them in.

We have to get out of middle school mentality that there isn't enough room at the lunch table. There's always room at the Lord's table. Scoot over and share your PB&J. Get outside of yourself and get a little uncomfortable. When you do, you'll find your world is fuller and more fulfilled when your arms are wide open.

You don't have to be best friends with everyone. But you can invite them into the body of Christ—it is our tribe. Ultimately, you will probably settle with a few close friends whom you can trust with your deepest struggles. These will be the ones who will give you godly advice, wise counsel, and consistent prayer. They will know your dirty little secrets and your consistent sins—and they'll love you anyway. Hold on to these saints.

But in all circumstances, be thoughtful. Smile. Be generous with your time and resources. Be sympathetic and compassionate. Look for opportunities to bake pumpkin bread for the neighbor, write a touching thank-you note, or stay late and help clean up.

And remember, when asked, people always say they are "fine," but they're not. So keep pressing in. When they realize you are sincerely curious and willing to engage, they will open up.

Be the friend you want someone else to be for you. Likewise, be the comforter Christ has been for you.

IDENTITY CRISIS

At the beginning of the chapter, we talked briefly about identity. But it's something we need to double-click on to make sure it sinks in. Having the right identity is critical for navigating a holy and purposeful life.

Too many of us are being defined by what we have, how we live, what we do, and where we go. However, identity is *who we are*. It is the compass that guides how we live our lives and what we do. In Galatians 2:20, Paul broke the cultural mindset and redefined how a believer should be identified. He stated, "I have been crucified with Christ and I no longer live, but Christ lives in me" (NIV).

This is a radical statement. Paul was saying, "I've willingly sacrificed my own passions, direction, and control so that Christ may take over. I no longer identify as Paul—I now identify solely as a disciple of Christ."

As a former medical professional, I took a lot of anatomy classes in school. So I've been intrigued by all the medical and technological advances we have seen the last few years, especially around DNA. For the first time, we are able to splice and replace genes to alter the traits of a human. While there are a lot of ethical questions outstanding, we can now alter things on the inside that will transform people on the outside.

The same holds true about our identity. When we submit our lives to Christ and allow Him to change us from the inside, our lives and actions are transformed on the outside.

When Jesus is grafted into our souls, He alters our identity so that we look more like Him. We become image-bearers of God, the *imago Dei*. The perfection that was Christ's now defines us. The love He poured out is now ours to give. The strength to press on, patience to withstand, and courage to holdfast are now tightly woven into the very fabric of our spiritual structure.

When our souls reflect the image of God…

We have this amazing ability to reason and choose, which is a reflection of God's intellect and freedom.

We become set apart and start walking in righteousness, which reflects God's holiness.

We embrace community, fellowship, and relationships, which is a beautiful reflection of the triune nature of God.

Our identity in Christ is a great Christian comfort, a soothing balm to heal our broken hearts, and a bridge across difficult circumstances. When we embrace our identity in Christ, we get to experience all the riches and gifts that come with it: knowledge, power, inheritance, hope, grace, and the Holy Spirit, just to name a few.

On the other hand, one of the greatest threats to our souls is identity misplacement. This is when we allow our identities to be defined by other things. Our enemy will do everything in his power to lie to you, dissuade you, and deceive you. He doesn't want to see God's goodness lived out in you. He wants to suppress you with distraction, comfort, and applause. He wants you to confuse happiness for joy, ease for contentment, and affirmation for acceptance. He knows he can't *change* your identity, but he can delude your mind and make you question it. He can render you useless and ineffective.

But…

When we understand that God has given us immeasurable greatness in His power, that our perfect identity is sealed with Jesus and expressed in the Holy Spirit, that we are redeemed from darkness to live freely as the light, that we are forgiven through the riches of His grace, that our once-blinded eyes are enlightened to see His eternal hope, that His rich mercy and great love have resurrected our lifeless souls to a new life—we should bravely and passionately rise to face each day.

We were made to courageously battle sin and walk in holiness. We aren't expected to be perfect—we are expected to live out God's perfection.

So take heart, dear sisters. Your heart, soul, and identity are forever safe in Jesus.

SURRENDERED EFFORT

Our identity and hope lie in Jesus. When Jesus yelled, "*Tetelestai*"—"It is finished" (John 19:30)—on the cross, our chains were snapped and we were set free.

We are free to embrace our awkward personalities. We don't have to say all the right things, wear the right clothes, or be the most popular. We are free not to fit in.

We are free from the need to prove anything. Christ already showed up and showed out when He was resurrected from the dead. It doesn't get more magnificent or miraculous than that.

We are free to engage in hard conversations, and we are free to be wrong, to be admonished, to be disciplined, and to learn and grow. We don't have to be afraid of the refining process. It's as iron sharpens iron, not as pillow fluffs pillow.

We are free to cheer and encourage one another, to stop competing and to start completing one another, because it's more about God than about us. The world will be shocked when we go out of our way to build others up.

We are free to say no. Activity does not always equate to progress, and busy doesn't always equal meaning. Some of your best memories will come when you planned nothing on a cool, Tuesday afternoon. It's okay to say no to one more school event or work party.

We are free to do impossibly difficult things and to fail time and time again. There are no Scripture verses on being remarkably successful, but a myriad on stepping out in faith and out of our comfort zones.

We are free from trying so hard to be perfect, pretty, and pleasing. Our perfections don't display Jesus—His power shines through in our weaknesses. Shiny and tidy lives are often chained to the prison of performance or conformity.

Someday we will get to see it all working together and working out. We will understand that He isn't asking for successful effort, but *surrendered effort*. That He's not asking for tidy lives, but trusting lives. I know it's crazy hard to comprehend right now when the baby won't sleep and the dog throws up for the umpteenth time, but one day we will fully know, even as we are fully known. As Paul tells us, "Now we see only a reflection as in a mirror; then we shall see face to face. Now I know in part; then I shall know fully, even as I am fully known" (1 Corinthians 13:12 NIV).

Woman of God, you are fully known. His identity is yours forever, your soul made in the very image of your Creator. With that knowledge, you can live with abandon, love without limitation, encourage without pretense, fail without devastation, and succeed without pride.

You will still have times when you are discouraged because of your weight, your house, or your husband. You may struggle with the chaos of life, when your peers get the job you wanted, or when the opportunity you hoped for doesn't happen. You will have disappointments and loneliness, faults, failures, hurts, and hang-ups. These are inevitable. But they don't define you.

When you are disappointed, frustrated, or angry, it is because you have believed in yourself. So despite what the most popular authors or speakers say, quit believing in yourself. Believe in God. When we strive and push with our own effort, we become exhausted and miss out on life. A spirit of striving is never from the Spirit of God.

J.C. Ryle once said, "It costs something to be a true Christian. Let that never be forgotten. To be a mere nominal Christian, and go to church, is cheap and easy work. But to hear Christ's voice, and follow Christ, and believe in Christ, and confess Christ, requires much self-denial."[1]

Sister, embrace your identity in Christ. Fight for holiness and a life that bears fruit. Slay the sin that is holding you down. You are a mighty woman of God, called to live risen. Accept nothing less.

This is who you are meant to be.

9

All the Things

He satisfies the longing soul, and the
hungry soul he fills with good things.

PSALM 107:9

remember the day my firstborn son turned one. I had it all planned
out, as every mother does with their first child. There would be big
celebration with all of his "friends," complete with a baby book full
of milestone pictures, an elaborate documentation of first words, and
a video slide show that would leave us all in a puddle of tears. Before
the party, I took him for professional pictures. It was going to be an
exciting day.

Until this point, he had never eaten anything with refined sugar.
His diet consisted primarily of green beans and rice cereal. (No judg-
ment. My third kid came out of the womb drinking chocolate milk.)
The time had come for him to finally taste the sweet manna known as
chocolate cake, and the photo session would capture this monumental occasion.

As I sat him down, the photographer readied herself to snap the
perfect shot of his blissful glee. I strategically lowered the cake right in

front of him, fully expecting him to dig in before the count of three. But what happened next shocked us all. Tears quickly formed in his eyes as he began to melt down in the most heart-wrenching cry.

I tried coaxing him to try the cake, wiping the frosting across his lip and sticking my chocolaty finger in his mouth, but he swiftly pulled away, madder than a wet hornet. Desperate to calm him down, I lifted him onto my lap. When I did, he reached for my purse. I knew what he wanted. He was looking for the bag of plain old Cheerios, his snack of choice. When I handed him a few, he immediately stopped crying.

Crazy, I thought. He could have had a slice of chocolate heaven covered in frosting, but instead he settled for a piece of cereal that tastes like cardboard. He had no idea what he was missing.

The same can be said about my life with Christ.

In my obstinacy, I often fight for what I want, for what is comfortable, and for my preconceived plans and dreams. I want control over my life, and even though God is speaking gently to me, I still resist. I don't trust the Maker of my soul. I don't trust that He wants what is best for me. I don't trust that life will go better for me if I listen to Him.

Women often approach me and tell me how their lives are on the brink of collapse. The stories are different, but the root cause is always the same—their souls are exhausted. Their souls aren't empty; they're stuffed. Their lives are so full of work trips, kids' events, and household duties that they don't have the time and capacity to grab ahold of what will truly fill, sustain, and nourish. They are rummaging for Cheerios, denying the very grace and joy our souls were meant to possess.

My soul is needy. And so is yours. This isn't a bad thing. In fact, God made our souls to desire and crave. But they will be satisfied with only one thing: the living water. Just like our cars won't run on queso or marshmallows, our souls won't run on anything but the Spirit of God.

In the days of Jeremiah, during the reign of King Josiah in Israel, God's chosen people had committed spiritual adultery. They had traded a trusting, living relationship with Yahweh for the love and worship of foreign, lifeless idols. They broke the covenant vows they had made with God that would ensure a protected blessing.

God told Jeremiah, "My people have committed two evils: they have forsaken me, the fountain of living waters, and hewed out cisterns for themselves, broken cisterns that can hold no water" (Jeremiah 2:13).

In those days, the Palestinians had three options for obtaining water. The best choice was from a source of fresh springs and streams nearby, referred to as *mayim khayyim,* or "living water." The second option was through a well that tapped into groundwater. The last choice was runoff water collected with a hewn cistern. With this method, silt and sludge would collect along with the water. If a cistern were to break, the water would seep out and leave nothing but muck.

If our souls are fed with anything but the living water, we are trying to survive on wet sludge. Jesus said, "If anyone thirsts, let him come to me and drink. Whoever believes in me, as the Scripture has said, 'Out of his heart will flow rivers of living water'" (John 7:37-38).

Not only is Jesus saying that we should come to Him, but that we should come to *drink.* We should drink in a wholehearted, personal, and abiding relationship with Him so that He can guide and sustain our souls. Jesus doesn't want us to just be converts. He wants us to be disciples. He wants us to walk next to Him, be sanctified through Him, and be satisfied with Him.

How many of us, if we are being completely honest, could say that Jesus has changed every aspect of our lives and continues to do so?

Many of us say we trust Jesus. We believe the resurrection story. We attend church on a regular basis. But we haven't surrendered. We are still crying for Cheerios. And this is why our lives haven't changed all that much. This is why we still feel so much angst and worry. This is why we continue to strive for more and try to find happiness in everything from food to sex.

The Hebrew word for soul is *nephesh.* The biblical writers describe the soul as a yearning, craving, and needy entity, never completely satisfied. In fact, *nephesh* is also translated as mouth or stomach. It is constantly hungry and thirsty.

John Ortberg explained the constant craving of the soul this way:

> My mind may be obsessed with idols; my will may be enslaved to habits; my body may be consumed with appetites. But my soul will never find rest until it rests in God. The paradox of the soul is that it is incapable of satisfying itself but it is also incapable of living without satisfaction.[1]

When the will has become enslaved by its need, when the mind has become obsessed with the object of its desire, when the appetite of the body has become a master rather than servant, the soul is disordered. The ultimate reality behind human dissatisfaction is sinful souls that have been cut off from the God we were made to rest in.

Our souls are hungry, and instead of filling them with holy and righteous portions that will nourish, we feed them junk food. We max out our calendars, pour another glass of wine, or eat an entire bag of potato chips. We binge on Netflix. We spend money we don't have. We sign our kids up for every possible extracurricular activity, chase the next raise, and spin at the gym. We throw every self-help food at our starving soul and it still longs for more.

Sisters, this is not to make you feel defeated or shamed. I struggle with the same things. This message is a wake-up call. It is supposed to shake us of our worthless habits and remind us that we are daughters of the King.

C.S. Lewis famously wrote,

> It would seem that Our Lord finds our desires not too strong, but too weak. We are half-hearted creatures, fooling about with drink and sex and ambition when infinite joy is offered us, like an ignorant child who wants to go on making mud pies in a slum because he cannot imagine

what is meant by the offer of a holiday at the sea. We are far too easily pleased.[2]

We are too easily pleased. And that constant longing in your life is your soul reminding you that you were made for so much more.

A WORSHIPPING SOUL

In chapter 3, we talked about worship and how we were created to be worshippers. Whether we are worshipping a pumpkin spice latte or our Savior, we are perpetually worshipping something at all times. What we worship is an indicator of our heart orientation and a sign of what is important to us.

This is the essence of what Jesus was explaining to Martha when she was upset that Mary was sitting as His feet instead of helping her entertain their guests. If we don't worship God, we will naturally find our affections and identity placed on something else. Sometimes we aren't even aware of the things that have captured our hearts and taken hold of our souls.

Maybe it's your marriage. You may have your spouse on the throne of your heart. It's easy to expect your husband to meet all your emotional and spiritual needs. But he wasn't designed to play this part. Husbands get distracted. They get angry. They get engulfed at work. They forget to hang the picture on the wall and pick the underwear off the floor. Even the best godly men will fail you because they are human. God created us as helpmates to our husbands because He knew they are awesome partners but terrible gods.

Maybe it's your desire to become a mother. You've waited and waited. You've prayed all the prayers. You've done the fast. You've read all the books. You've even made a few deals with God while spending your life savings on pregnancy tests, hoping for two blue lines. You're starting to wonder if God even cares.

I don't understand all the mysteries of God, but I do know He doesn't want any desire—no matter how good—consuming you and stealing your joy. If He has you in a season of waiting, He may be trying to reveal something to you—a purpose and calling already in front of you.

Maybe it's your kids. If your kid's football game, volleyball tournament, piano recital, or report card brings you overwhelming joy, you may be worshipping the wrong thing. Children are a blessing and a sweet gift, but your identity cannot be based on their accomplishments. When we place our worth on them, we "worthship" them and their achievements. And the worst part is that they have embraced their deity status. Why do you think much of the younger generation acts entitled and spoiled? We have placed them on an elevated pedestal.

Maybe it's your dream, your job, or your hobbies. I can quickly become irritated at the smallest inconvenience, especially when it interrupts my productivity or daily plan. When I'm preparing for a talk, I'm quick to snap at the kids for playing music, roll my eyes when Bear needs to go out, or act put out when Jason asks a question. It's because my plan is of ultimate importance at that time.

That's sad. And it explains how I'm quick to worship my priorities, even at the cost of those souls around me. I'm guessing you have your own examples of when you get in the way of God. When our jobs and dreams hold too much weight, they can suffocate or paralyze us. They consume our thoughts, overwhelm our time, and steal our joy.

It's easy to worship those tangible things around us. And it's easy to get lost in the pursuit of these things for your entire life. But your soul is crying out for something more.

A DIVIDED SOUL

I remember a conflict I had with Jason early in our marriage. It was the kind you look back on and wonder why or how you even got to that ridiculous place of losing your mind and all sense of control. Sadly I can't even remember what started the fight. But I do remember hours and hours of frustrated and defensive bickering, which only escalated our emotions and anger.

This particular fight ended with me withdrawing and driving away in my car. This was highly unusual for me. I'm usually the pursuer in our conflicts, following Jason from room to room in an attempt to continue conversation even when a little space would make more sense. So for me to walk away indicated I had hit my limit.

In the midst of this particular conflict, I remember thinking I shouldn't be saying the things I was saying. The conversation felt strangely surreal, like I was outside of myself, shaking my head in amazement at the words coming out of my mouth.

In my mind, I was thinking, *You don't mean that. Don't you dare walk away. Hug him now. Right now. Keep going...you can do this. No! Turn back around. Don't roll your eyes at him. Move toward him. Put your arm around him. Think of all of the wonderful things about him and thank him. Or at least thank God for them. Yes, there is at least one thing you love about him.* In retrospect, I'm certain it wasn't my voice. It was the Holy Spirit wrestling for me.

A war is waging within us. Our souls are easily divided as the passions of our flesh and the sin that easily entangles are in daily combat with the Spirit that works powerfully within us. In relational conflict, the real enemy is not my husband, but my fallen nature.

Jason and I made up later that night. But it took a while for both of us stubborn sinners to surrender, to lean into God's presence, and to allow the Holy Spirit to speak to us. In the heat of battle, we wanted to win, conquer, and control—but we ultimately recognized that the relationship with each other and Christ was more important.

The apostle Paul was a man of great worldly accomplishment. Before coming to Christ, he was living a life directed by his fallen nature. He was a performer and an achiever. He desired recognition and success. But God captured his heart and redirected it. After an encounter with Jesus, his soul was reset. He was still a hard driver and an activator, but those strong traits were redirected to serving Christ and serving others. He surrendered his fallen flesh.

Dysfunction of the soul isn't a problem of division, but of order. We prioritize and emphasize the wrong things. There is nothing wrong with buying a new shirt, playing sports, earning a degree, or wanting to hustle for your business…as long as these things are sanctified by the Word and prayer. "Everything created by God is good, and nothing is to be rejected if it is received with thanksgiving, for it is made holy by the word of God and prayer" (1 Timothy 4:4-5).

They have to be in the right order. Our sin nature must submit to the Holy Spirit.

The reason Paul highlighted thanksgiving, the Word of God, and prayer was because they reestablish order. They put God first. When we are thankful, we honor the Giver. Thanksgiving is a powerful antidote to worry and fear. The Word of God refocuses us back to the Bible and reminds us to seek His guidance. And prayer creates solitude, drowns out the worldly noise, and reestablishes an intimate connection to Christ.

God never asks us to remove all the things that fight for position in our hearts. But He does command us, first and foremost, to live faithfully and obediently, holding fast to His promises. He knew we would be distracted by the things of this world. So He gave us the Word of God to remind us how to live.

At times we have to take extreme measures to keep order. We have to implement boundaries and put ourselves in the best possible position to successfully wage war against the passions that compete for our lives. We must learn to depend on God so that we can hold this tension between the extremes.

But our souls do not need to be divided. If we are submitted to

Christ, we can integrate the appetites of the body, the focus of the mind, and the desires of the heart into a place of great peace and satisfaction.

A HUNGRY SOUL

If you're not filling your soul with the fullness of God, you're going to be constantly hungry, perpetually parched, and never completely satisfied. But when the living water quenches our souls, we are refreshed, recharged, and satisfied. We then begin to overflow. We can pour out to others. We go from spent to well spent and from chasing perfect to living within Christ's perfection.

The Lord reminded Isaiah of this when He said, "If you pour yourself out for the hungry and satisfy the desire of the afflicted, then shall your light rise in the darkness and your gloom be as the noonday. And the Lord will guide you continually and satisfy your desire" (Isaiah 58:10-11).

I recently read an interesting study that assessed the link between people with food-related hardships and obesity.[3] Initially, I didn't understand how an overweight person could possibly be hungry. Wouldn't obesity indicate an abundance of food? What research revealed was that many people are not always hungry for calories; they are hungry for nutrition. They are often too poor to afford foods that will nurture their bodies, maintain their weight, and balance their caloric and energy levels. The poor often eat foods that are high in carbohydrates and fat instead of dense, cell-satisfying nutrients. Their stomachs are full, but their bodies are empty. This has led to a significant obesity crisis, not to mention an increase in diabetes and heart-related problems.

We have a hunger crisis with our souls as well. Our lives are full, but our souls are ravenously hungry. Our fullness is deceiving so most people don't realize it. We are empty, complacent, and apathetic. We have eaten so much junk that we've lost our taste for God.

Paul told the Philippian church that he had learned a great mystery, the secret to contentment. He learned to be content in all circumstances, whether having plenty or being in need. He said, "I can do all things through [Christ] who strengthens me" (Philippians 4:13).

This is one of the most misrepresented verses in the entire Bible. It is often used as a motivational quote to help athletes fight for victory or to encourage people to be overcomers. While I appreciate the sentiment, I doubt Paul was hoping his words would help Stephen Curry win another NBA championship.

The proper context is that through Christ, we have the capacity to be satisfied in all circumstances. Jesus gives us the strength to be content. Regardless of our external circumstances, we can have internal peace. Even if your spouse dies, your children rebel, your boss fires you, your health fades, or your dreams crumble, you can have inner joy. Write that on a coffee mug!

The content soul remains unwavered by suffering and hardship or blessings and successes. It is unchanged by circumstance, because satisfaction isn't gleaned from the outside. Contentment comes from the ever-present, unconditional, all-consuming love and grace of God *within* us. The daily consumption of God's Word and intimacy with the loving Father is what fills us and satisfies us.

I remember the bittersweet process of sleep training my babies. Our doctor recommended the cry-it-out method, which encourages parents to let the baby cry until she falls asleep when she's full with milk and has a clean diaper. This was tough. A real punch in the mom-gut. It's hard to listen to your child crying in her crib, longing to be held by her momma. But I knew my babies had all they needed to be content and satisfied. They just had to learn to operate in uncomfortable external circumstances.

We have to learn this too. We are spiritual babies, and once God has empowered us with all we need for life and godliness, we can live free and full of joy. But freedom doesn't mean independence. In fact, it's just the opposite. Our life mission should not be self-sufficiency, but complete dependency and reliance on God.

Mild stress and strategic disappointment can be beneficial to the soul when it causes us to depend more on God. Sometimes we need to be broken so that we can learn about delayed gratification. Sometimes we need others to be in the spotlight so that we can learn to applaud, encourage, and cheer for their success. Sometimes our expectations need to be unmet so that we will develop a contrite and humble spirit. As God said to Isaiah, "This is the one to whom I will look: he who is humble and contrite in spirit and trembles at my word" (Isaiah 66:2).

> Freedom doesn't mean independence. In fact, it's just the opposite.

A hungry soul, when taught to feed on the Word of God, teaches us to love God more. And we need to love God more. We need to love God more than applause, more than being right, more than defending our position, more than career success, more than extravagant trips, more than close friends, more than decadent food, more than fashionable clothes, and more than comfortable homes.

I don't always do this well. There are times when I want both, which means my soul is already out of whack. But deep down, I want to love God more. Because I know my hungry soul can only find true satisfaction in Him.

A CHARGED SOUL

As I mentioned earlier, I'm addicted to my iPhone. If I'm not careful, my phone can easily become an unhealthy source of distraction that consumes my days and my moments. I'm afraid to know how much time I've wasted staring at my screen and checking notifications.

If I were only this addicted to God. What if I...

Checked in with Him regularly.

Was constantly alert for notifications and necessary updates from Him.

Desired His likes.

Struggled to put Him down.

Checked all my directions with Him, knowing I'd be lost without Him.

Searched for answers to all of my daily questions in His Word.

Made Him the last check-in at night and the first check-in in the morning.

Captured all my precious moments with Him.

Found joy in connecting others to Him.

Carried Him wherever I went.

When we are not continuously connected to Christ, then, like our iPhones, we quickly start losing our charge. We have to be connected to the ultimate source of power. Our spiritual batteries start running low when we try to handle life on our own, and this is what leads to our inner depletion.

My son thought he knew best when he chose Cheerios over chocolate cake. But his mommy knew better. She knew what she had in store for him, and she knew how much better it would be if he would just trust her.

Sisters, our heavenly Daddy knows. He's just waiting for us to trust Him.

10

Rare Love

> You shall love the Lord your God with all
> your heart and with all your soul and with
> all your mind. This is the great and first
> commandment. And a second is like it: You
> shall love your neighbor as yourself.
>
> **MATTHEW 22:37-39**

During my first year in college, I struggled with an eating disorder. I don't remember how it started, but I'm certain it was fueled by my desire for attention from the college boys. I bought into the lie that being thin is the perfect body type, and I spiraled down from there. Most sin is a slow, numbing dissent, often masked in good intentions, and my struggle was no exception.

The healthy rhythms of eating, resting, and moving were replaced with an overwhelming and consuming desire to control every minute and moment of my day. My mind was consumed with what I ate, how much I ran, and the number on the scale. The lies I believed burrowed deep into my heart and began consuming me.

I have never felt more trapped than in that season of life. Controlled and enslaved, I was chained to the death cage of my own sin. Food wasn't the sin. My sin was trying to find acceptance and identity in myself, my appearance, and the approval of others. I looked to everyone but God. I didn't believe God's approval was enough.

I know many of us struggle with eating disorders. Anorexia, bulimia, and gluttony are issues that plague many of us in this externally focused society. If you have ever eaten an entire box of Thin Mints or grabbed a Big Mac on the way home from work, I get it. It's a stress reliever. It makes you feel good. It's an immediate fix with instant gratification. We like the instant satisfaction food brings to us when we are emotionally and physically exhausted.

Both anorexia and gluttony are fruit problems, not root problems. In other words, these eating disorders are the external manifestations of our inner turmoil. The root problem is idolatry, giving food more power than God. Withholding food is a mark of seeking control and the approval of man, of chasing the perfect body. Overindulging in food seeks to numb the stress or pain of life. But the things we numb out on will never satisfy the hunger of the soul. Only complete, radical dependence on Him can give you the security, acceptance, and peace you seek.

I vividly remember the knock on my bedroom door. It was my dad. I was living at home during my first years of college, and my eating disorder had become evident to everyone in the family. Dad had come to talk because he had witnessed the battle I was fighting and suspected I was losing. He was right, even without the knowledge of the empty cereal boxes hiding under my bed, the fast food remnants stashed in my car, and the vicious cycles of starvation and purging.

I was trembling, tired, and afraid. I wasn't afraid of my dad, but I was utterly exhausted from both the mental and physical strain. I wanted to be released from the disorder so badly, but I was afraid of the cost. I felt trapped in my own body. This is what sin does. It takes God's perfect creation and warps it. It takes sex and makes it lust. It takes worship and makes it idolatry. And it takes a provision like food and makes it an obsession.

My dad has always been there for me. He loves me more than himself. Growing up, he constantly did without so that the family could have more. He gave of his time, his energy, and his resources. He preached the gospel, but he taught us even more by how he lived. He was the message. So as I sat on my bed in tears, I knew his very presence was an act of love, even if it brought my painful secret to the light.

When he walked in the room, his posture was both merciful and serious. My dad is known to be clear and direct, and he was staying true to form for this meeting. After a few platitudes, he told me he loved me and it was time we conquered this eating problem. And then he said if I wasn't ready to tackle the problem I would have to move out.

I was stunned. How could he do that? How could such an amazing, kind, and selfless father turn his child away? Wouldn't that be the very worst thing? Didn't he know I needed him more than ever? If I left, I would be fighting this battle away from the protection of his roof.

As we talked further and I cried, I began to realize what he meant by "it was time." It was time for me to draw a line in the sand. I had been playing with this sin struggle instead of identifying it, calling it out, asking for help, and putting together a plan to recover. I said I wanted to heal, but I hadn't taken any of the necessary steps to get on the path to freedom. And my dad knew it. He knew I needed to feel the full weight of my sickness or I'd never really fight against it. He loved me enough to tell me the truth. In love.

This kind of love is rare. Most of the "love" you hear about in the media is a bastardized and dangerous version that allows anyone to do whatever they want, regardless of the consequences. Our society often describes love as a giant group hug where all participants are free to do whatever feels right to them. But that isn't love at all. Love is speaking truth to one another in gentleness. Love is facing the hard issues with a soft heart and open hands. Love is drawing lines in the sand, like

Jesus did when He was brought the woman caught in adultery and He offered forgiveness. But He also told her to go and sin no more. He loved her enough to call her actions what they were—sin. Lines in the sand can be weighty.

According to 1 Corinthians 13, rare love is tender and gentle. It is patient and kind. It does not keep a record of wrongs. Rare love doesn't boast or insist on its own way. Rare love is not irritable or resentful. It bears and believes and hopes and endures all things.

When I was neck-deep in my addiction, I mistakenly thought my father's love should project only consolation and sympathy. The problem with this viewpoint is that it assumes only the soft attributes are needed to redeem and restore brokenness, which is not the case. Hard and truthful conversations married with support, wisdom, understanding, and encouragement are needed.

It would not be loving for a cardiologist to tell a patient that "everything is going to be just fine" when the person has a massive blockage in the crucial arteries that supply blood to the heart. It would also not be loving to hand him a Band-Aid or give him a high five. The guy needs major heart surgery. He needs someone to tell him he's a ticking time bomb. He needs immediate intervention. Of course, doing that isn't easy, but it's what is best for the patient. It's love expressing itself in complete truth, surrounded with encouragement, refinement, and realignment.

My father loved me enough to expose the truth about my addiction. The truth was hard to hear, but it shone a light on my sin and forced me to face it. And because I did, I eventually recovered. But had my dad just "loved" me the way the world teaches us to love—allowing us to do whatever we want—I might not be here today.

RARE LOVE IS SACRIFICIAL

Sacrifice is a misunderstood word.

If I buy a homeless man a meal in addition to my own meal, that is being thoughtful. But if I buy a homeless man a meal *instead* of buying one for myself, that is sacrifice. Thoughtful gestures are different from actual sacrifice. Genuine and authentic sacrifice is exceptionally rare. It is pure love that places another's needs above your own.

Sacrifice isn't comfortable, which is why most people don't practice it. Fortunately for us, our Lord and Savior, Jesus Christ, was willing to be uncomfortable. He was willing to be flogged, humiliated, and nailed to a cross. He was willing to give the ultimate sacrifice, His life, for ours. As Jesus said in John 15:13, "Greater love has no one than this: to lay down one's life for one's friends" (NIV).

I didn't see it at the time, but my dad practiced sacrificial love as well. He was willing to sacrifice a short-term relationship with me. He was willing to go through the pain of watching his oldest daughter angrily move out of the house. He was willing to sacrifice an undefined amount of time with me for me to heal. As long as I had the provision and protection of home, he knew I wouldn't feel the need to lean on Jesus. This was an act of faith by my father, trusting God would hold me. Now that I have my own kids, I get it. Sometimes you must do the hard thing to help your kids find their way home. Rare love is sacrificial. But it's also radical.

Instead of saying, "You can't love others until you love yourself," we should be saying, "You can't love others until you *forget* yourself."

The greatest self-love is to love God above self. The best thing you can do for yourself is to get over yourself. Those with the greatest amount of love are the ones who empty themselves willingly and readily. When no one is watching and when there is no hidden or ulterior motive, radical love leaps out in faith and sacrifices resources and time. It demonstrates a life completely stripped of self.

Too often we don't believe God will show up for us if we do risky, radical things. We don't believe His solution will be better. We don't believe He will manifest Himself in miraculous ways. We have the head knowledge about God, but it doesn't translate into actions for our hands and feet.

I often wonder if God is just waiting for us. He wants to show up. He wants to prove His faithfulness. He wants to prove that He is enough, that He hears us, that He understands the desires of our heart. He wants to demonstrate His sufficiency to meet all our needs. But we have to present the need. We have to give Him the opportunity to be big. We have to take a leap of faith.

> Instead of saying, "You can't love others until you love yourself," we should be saying, "You can't love others until you *forget* yourself."

But taking that leap is uncomfortable.

Fortunately, we aren't called to a comfortable life—we are called to an abundant life. Francis Chan pleaded to all of us when he said, "God doesn't call us to be comfortable. He calls us to trust Him so completely that we are unafraid to put ourselves in situations where we will be in trouble if He doesn't come through."[1]

I like that. Unafraid. Rare love is unafraid to try, to fail, and to practice love in radical and sacrificial ways.

It's not a group hug. It's better.

RARE LOVE IS TOUGH

The heart of God longs to bring His people back to Himself, to redeem hearts that are prone to wander. We are rebels who keep rejecting the way that is best. We are prodigals who constantly set out on our own. We naturally yoke to sin instead of holiness. And sin is what is sucking the life out of our souls.

But the heart of the Father is always restoration. Jesus calls sinners to repentance, which forces us to recognize the seriousness of sin but frees us when we accept the grace offered to us.

Restoration always requires truth. Truth is the bedrock of love. And love is the catalyst for grace. If we remove one component of restoration, truth, love, or grace from the equation, we have only a frilly sentiment or a cute Hallmark card. We have no power. Without restoration, we are separated from the Father. Without truth, we are blind to our sins. Without love, we have selfishly absorbed hearts. And without grace, we are trapped in our transgressions. God redeems us as He applies His tough love to our lives.

When my dad called me out on my eating disorder, he admitted me to the operating room. I didn't need a pep talk. I needed heart surgery. I needed to come face-to-face with the hard truth and walk down a rough road to remedy the problem. It required an active saving faith, not just a saying faith.

If God truly loves us—and if our Christian brothers and sisters truly love us—then we must apply tough love to our relationships.

Tough love isn't a license to hammer those around you. It is the wise and discerning application of unconditional love in difficult circumstances. Jesus came for the sick, not the healthy. Likewise, we are called to minister and love those who are lost and lonely. The difficult part is accepting people regardless of the choices they make, separating the sinner from the sin. A person is not the sum total of their sins. Every person is made in the image of God, and their sin nature is simply a reflection of decisions made apart from Him. Despite what culture may shout online, you can accept a person and not their destructive life patterns.

My dad fully accepted me. He loved me. But he didn't accept the choices I was making that were damaging my body and soul.

If you run in Christian circles, you've probably heard the mantra, "We should live *in truth and love*." While we mean well with this saying, it is a bit misleading. Truth is a part of love. So it would be more accurate to say, "We should *demonstrate truth in love*."

Over and over throughout Scripture, Jesus demonstrated truth in love. He demonstrated it when He invited a despised tax collector, Zacchaeus, to dinner. He demonstrated it when He healed the man with leprosy who was calling out His name. He demonstrated it when He told the repentant thief on the neighboring cross that he would be with Him that day in paradise. Jesus constantly demonstrated truth in love. And He did it intentionally. These weren't random acts of kindness—these were intentional and purposeful demonstrations of love, displayed in truth and grace.

But not everyone accepts the Truth.

Jesus also said He came to bring the sword. He knew His words would divide. They would split relationships. Families would take sides. He knew the truth would be tough to hear—and even tougher to live—and that most people would rather rely on their own feelings.

> The heart of the Father is always restoration.

Ultimately, the problem is that we are called to be perfect as our heavenly Father is perfect. And the truth is that it is impossible to attain perfection unless Christ steps in and takes our place. If we want Christ to take our place, then we have to voluntarily step out of the way. We have to cede control. We have to be servants. This is tough to hear for most people.

But the good news sets us free. Even when we fail, we are loved. Even when we mess up, we are found worthy. When we trust God is enough, we can love dangerously. We can live bravely. We can be intentional. We can have peace. And we can demonstrate a rare love that expresses truth and reveals grace.

TENDING THE SOUL

Accepting Christ wholeheartedly frees us to love others rightly. We don't have to love them from a position of need or acceptance. We don't have to worry over whether they like us. We can see differences as opportunities to grow. We can embrace things we don't understand. We can encourage one another instead of ignoring or comparing. We begin to see people for what's on the inside and not what's on the outside.

In 1 Corinthians 13, the Greek word for love is *agape*. It is the deepest form of love and the kind God displayed by sacrificing Himself on the cross. *Agape* love involves faithfulness, commitment, and an act of the will. It is different from the other forms of love mentioned in the New Testament—erotic love and brotherly love—because of its moral nature and strong character. It seeks the benefit of the ones it loves. It is not based on feelings, but on one's will and commitment.

True *agape* love is truth spoken from a charitable place, a place that is seeking the good of another. *Agape* love does not speak down to others, nor does it speak in arrogance or unrighteous judgement. It speaks with tenderness and genuine humility.

When Paul admonished the churches, he did so with tears. He was broken for them. His genuine concern ran so deep that it pulled out real emotions. He shared this same sentiment in his teaching in Titus 3:2-3 when he said, "To avoid quarreling, to be gentle, to show perfect courtesy [gentleness and meekness] toward all people. For we ourselves were once foolish, disobedient, led astray, slaves to various passions and pleasures."

Paul understood that an arrogant and harsh correction rarely heals and softens hearts. It is not a reflection of *agape* love. A surgeon is effective when she prefaces her work with anesthesia to numb the pain and then uses a scalpel, not a hatchet. Likewise, we need to approach others with a gentle and compassionate heart, just as our gentle Shepherd comes to us. He has dealt with our souls in tenderness with great compassion, and we need to do the same with others.

Viewing it through the lens of *agape* love, it is worth revisiting Jesus's teaching in Luke 10:27: "Love the Lord your God with all your heart and with all your soul and with all your strength and with all your mind."

With all your heart...

The heart is the seat of our affections and desires. God doesn't just want our intellectual assent or rote service. He wants our heart. He wants us to pursue Him, seek Him, and find joy in Him.

If you are feeling constantly distracted by the daily activities and worries of life, there's a good chance you aren't loving God with all your heart. When I fell in love with Jason, I thought about him all the time, looked for ways to please him, longed to be with him, and experienced excitement with him. And I still do. I gave my heart to him.

Have you given your heart to God?

With all your soul...

When God calls us to *agape* with our soul, He asks us to love Him with our entire being. If you remember what we discussed earlier, the soul is the integrator of the heart, mind, and body. Loving God with our soul means we *agape* Him with our entire being and essence.

This is a daily choice you have to make and commit to. Most people dedicate a few hours on Sunday morning to worship God and some sprinkle in a little more time with Him throughout the week, but a fully devoted soul basks in God's presence continuously. Our souls need the constant nourishment that comes from above, and a devoted life thinks of Christ like breathing or eating.

With all your strength...

Loving God with all your strength refers to dedicating your body to Him. Our bodies were created with purpose and intent, a beautiful design in form and function. We honor and love God when we use them as He designed them in gender, sexuality, and function.

God describes our bodies as temples, which is a bold and magnificent statement. The temple in the Bible was the dwelling place of God. In other words, we get to house God in our flesh. What a privilege and responsibility to *agape* God in this way.

Our bodies are also a resource to steward. When we exercise and eat right, we allow our vessels the best opportunity to display and pour out the grace and truth of God. Our bodies allow us to fulfill the Great Commission—to go and make disciples of the nations. Our bodies may tire and change over time, but God gives us the needed strength for where we are.

With all your mind...

As women, we often struggle to love God with all our minds. We long for intimacy and feel-good emotions that come with a heart love, but we can sometimes miss devoting our minds to Him. But to know God intimately, we must know Him accurately. We must dig deeper to grasp a more robust understanding of theology and truth. We should be just as diligent in loving Him with our minds as we do with our hearts. As Jen Wilkin says, "The heart can't love what the mind doesn't know."[2]

We are far too easily satisfied with bite-sized, feel-good devotionals. We want others to spoon-feed us. We want to watch a 15-minute video. We don't take the time to read and study the Word of God.

But transformation begins with a renewing of the mind. If we are going to *agape* God, we have to know Him. And to know God, we have to engage with the page—dive deep into the Bible. This is how we are renewed and refreshed.

Reading the Bible is not something to do. It is someone to become. When we understand His character and nature in our minds, it begins to be displayed in all aspects of our lives.

Just a week ago, my youngest son, Rogue, got out of the car when I dropped him off at school and yelled, "Mommy, I love you to forever and back!" I told him I loved him more. He smiled a big toothless grin and ran off to class. I sat there for a few minutes and let his words sink in. It was a good moment and I wanted to remember it.

I know there will be a day in the near future when I'll be lucky if he waves. And then a day when he won't want me to drive him to the front door. And then a day when I won't have to.

It goes fast, so *agape* your kids big.

God wants us to love Him big as well. He doesn't just want a short wave or a muffled good-bye. He wants an all-out, toothless, reckless love that shouts from the cheap seats. He wants a passionate and public expression that doesn't care what others think. And He deserves it. He pulled me out of an eating disorder and gave me a healthy life. But more importantly, He pulled me out of debilitating sin and gave me a healthy soul. He released me from my shackles and set me on a path to freedom. He can do the same for you. God's love may be exceptional and exceptionally rare, but it is never limited. He gives in abundance. So seek it, receive it, be changed by it—and pass it on.

11

Keeping It Real

Now we see in a mirror dimly, but then face to
face; now I know in part, but then I will know
fully just as I also have been fully known.

1 CORINTHIANS 13:12 NASB

like garage sales. Actually, it's a serious obsession. I love finding them, shopping them, even having them. I don't care for the pricing, sorting, and negotiating, but the payoff of purging all the unused stuff around our house makes me want to floss like a boss.

Decluttering the outside of my life often makes the inside feel less cluttered as well. And who doesn't love a good deal? It doesn't matter that you already own three pairs of ripped jeans when you spot another pair for a dollar. And who doesn't need an extra scooter to take up space in the garage?

We recently had one of these big events. Yes, they officially become an event when weeks are spent preparing and planning. One of my goals was to sort through and discard all of the unnecessary toys and clothes that had been accumulating in my kids' bedrooms.

I've been told a rolling stone gathers no moss, but that can't be the case. Our family is rolling like a boulder down a steep hill and we are accumulating meaningless stuff all over the place. A plastic McDonald's toy here and a whistling birthday party favor there, and before you know it, you have your own mini Dollar Tree store.

Of course, if you try to trash or confiscate any of these unused plastic toys while your kids are in the room, they immediately become your child's most treasured possession. It makes no difference that it hasn't been played with since it was bought in the grocery line nine summers ago. At that moment, it is their absolute, most favorite toy in the history of the world. And to sell it would be to commit an unforgivable sin.

So, to get my children to participate in the great purge, I had to up my parenting game. I had to bribe them. Don't judge. I am not past a good bribe in the name of cleaning house.

My sneaky tactic worked. Sage dumped out half of her dresser, which was full of Shopkins, Squishys, and L.O.L. dolls. Since I told her I'd split the profits with her, she was extremely motivated. And it turned out her toys were highly desirable at the garage sale.

After the sale was over, Sage surprised me by saying she wanted to take some of her money and purchase a diary. At first, I was adamant with the kids that the money they made be saved. But when I heard she wanted a safe place to journal her intimate thoughts and prayers with God, I couldn't help but support her.

After sifting through hundreds of options, Sage landed on one that could only be unlocked with her voice. I kid you not. If either of her brothers tried to crack it open, the diary would say in a snarky, Alexa-type voice, "Caught you! Girls rule."

You can't make this stuff up.

She was so giddy to have her own diary, and it made my heart smile. When I was a little girl, I remember wanting the same thing. I wanted to process my inner thoughts in a safe place. I wanted to write out all of my feelings and struggles and not let anyone into my little world. I still journal at times, and it allows me to process things in a healthy but protected way. I was happy for her to have that outlet.

Later that week I was tucking her into bed at night when she pulled out her diary. With wide eyes and an eager expression, she pulled me close to tell me she wanted to share something. Much to my surprise, she began reading what she had written. I was all ears. Not because I wanted to hear her deepest secrets, but because I wanted her to feel safe with me. I wanted to be her diary.

As I walked up the stairs after our precious mommy-daughter time, I grinned, thinking how pointless it was to have a silly lock if she was going to divulge all her secrets anyway. But then it hit me. She wanted to be fully known.

We all want to be fully known. And loved just the way we are. Deep down, we all struggle with various sins, hang-ups, addictions, and temptations, but we don't want to be defined by them. We desperately want to know there are people who care about us and love us unconditionally. Our closest friends don't have to accept our biggest struggles, brokenness, and fears—in fact, they shouldn't if they really love us the way Christ does—but they should accept us as broken vessels.

Too many of us live in CPM—Constant Protection Mode. We silence our voice in fear of being demonized. We suppress our love in fear of being rejected. We ignore our calling in fear of being misunderstood. We are constantly trying to protect ourselves, and it is exhausting. We feel empty because we are not fully known by those around us.

When we desire the approval of others, it is especially easy to fall into CPM. We want to avoid conflict and please those around us. It may seem that we are close to others, but a lack of transparency really keeps others at a distance. They never see the real you. The truth is locked up, just like my daughter's diary.

Some people appear to "have it all together." But they rarely do. In fact, those who look polished and perfect often have a starving soul.

They think it's too risky to be authentic, but in reality, it's too risky not to be.

Deep down, we all want to be like the diary. Unlocked. Authentic. Fully known. We want people to see us in our broken relationship, with a troubled past, struggling to make ends meet. We want people to see us with the filters off, makeup in disarray, teeth unbrushed, and hair tangled. Actually, we need to brush our teeth. No excuse for that.

Have you been around people who aren't afraid to share their messy homes or current struggles without hesitation? Do those people make you feel better or worse? Do you have more respect for them or less? Do you want to be their friend?

To me, these people are like a breath of free air. I long to spend more time with them. I want to be like them.

These people have taught me an important truth: freed people free people.

Free people make you feel welcome. They welcome you into their homes, into their hearts, and into their imperfect lives. Because they don't pretend to have it all together, they give you the freedom to come as you are—bruised, battered, and broken. They like tidy, but they are not obsessed with it. They don't ignore their sins, but they are not defined by them either. They don't expect perfection, from themselves or others.

Free people live with authenticity, transparency, and vulnerability, which is why they experience the abundant life.

These three words have become buzzwords in social and ministry circles and are often used interchangeably. But they are different expressions of being real and being free.

Let's take a look.

BEING AUTHENTIC

Authenticity is the truthfulness of *what* you share and *who* you are. If Reign claimed he single-handedly scored three touchdowns in the last two minutes of his football game, I would hesitate to believe his authenticity. He's a good athlete, but that's a bit far-fetched, even for a woman of faith and a biased mom. I would probably request some video footage to validate his claim, which would only be authentic if proven legitimate.

Even though we often use the term *authentic* for designer purses or ethnic restaurants, authenticity is a key element of a believer's soul. Because authenticity is inextricably tied to truthfulness and because truthfulness is embodied in Christ, Christians should always desire to be authentic. It should be who we are.

The more I talk to women, the more I realize how exhausted we are with fakeness. *Pretense empties the soul.* Yet most people live their lives on social media and in the public doing some degree of acting. If you scroll through Instagram or Facebook, you'll see hundreds of pictures of beach vacations, fancy-schmancy restaurants, exotic concerts, and popular sporting events. Rarely do we see a story about a mom genuinely wrestling through what God would have her do with a wandering teen or an unfulfilling marriage.

Life feels staged. We know it, but for the sake of vanity and entertainment, we continue to participate in the nonsense. A popular hashtag lately has been #livingmybestlife and, of course, social media is full of all the things money can buy tagged to it. But for the Christian, our best life is yet to come, when all things will be made new. We should be authentic about the tough realities of this life, knowing the hope and joy we have coming in eternity. *That* will be our best life.

How do you know if you are being authentic? Let me pose some heart-check questions. Do you act the same offline as you do online? Do you respond differently to your husband than you do to a person at the gym? Do you turn into a different person the moment you walk out of church? These questions aren't meant to judge but to gauge. We can't become the people God calls us to be if we aren't realistic about who we are today.

Most women don't allow their inner light to come shining through because they are afraid. We are afraid no one will like us for the ordinary, aging, impatient, awkward, and uninteresting people we can often be. We are afraid people won't overlook our meltdowns and mess-ups, our flabby baby belly, and our disorganized family. We cringe at the thought of putting ourselves out there because rejection hurts. It feels too risky.

> For the Christian, our best life is yet to come, when all things will be made new.

But our confidence should be in God. He is where our identity lies. He is where our peace resides. He is our perfection.

As a child of God, we can risk. We don't have to worry about what others think. We can be the broken, imperfect mess we are and know we are fully rescued, redeemed, and restored before the One who loved us so much that He died for us. He brings perfect peace. And it's important to remember that He doesn't leave us in that broken mess.

It takes courage to accept our own imperfection and embrace our gifted perfection in Christ. Authenticity is a gateway to freedom, not only for yourself, but also for others. Living authentically is being the true you in all aspects of your life. It tears down walls and lowers shields. It's contagious. When we stop trying to cover up, we allow others to see God's love working through us, His grace forgiving us, and His power compelling us.

This is what it means to keep it real.

BEING TRANSPARENT

If authenticity is the truthfulness of *what* you share, then transparency is *how much* you share. It's the quantity of information. You can be completely transparent, but if you are not being authentic, then people are just getting more of your fabricated life, not your real story. I often hear people say, "I'm being completely transparent with you," as if sharing more is an acceptable substitute for sharing truth. As believers, we are called to be both real and open, authentic and transparent, so that others can experience the hope we have in relation to the troubles we face.

If I say I have an amazing husband most of the time, I am being authentic in that statement. However, I am not being fully transparent. I left out the fact that he leaves clothes on the chair indefinitely and puts his dirty shoes on the kitchen counter. And I also left out that he listens to me when he's tired, takes care of the kids when I'm overwhelmed, and operates as my personal masseuse when I'm stressed.

Most people have a governor on their transparency so that you know enough, but not too much. It's fashionable to share a few of our problems so that others recognize that we are introspective. But most people won't share the really hard stuff, because the really hard stuff exposes our deep-rooted inadequacies. But here's the catch and the mystery of God: our deep-rooted inadequacies expose our need for a Savior, namely Jesus Christ. The sins, addictions, and vices make it all the more obvious that we need a God who saves.

Those who are transparent offer more specifics and more information, which increases trust. We trust those who are open with us. We should be wise in how, when, and to what extent we are transparent with others, but we do need to share. I always tell my kids that the more authentic and transparent they are with me, the more freedoms I will grant them. I think the same sentiment applies to our souls. The more authentic and transparent we are, the freer we will be.

BEING VULNERABLE

Vulnerability may be the most difficult element of being real with people. It leaves you exposed. When you are truly vulnerable, you carry a risk of rejection, judgement, or attack. You can be authentic and transparent without being vulnerable, although genuine authenticity and transparency often require an element of vulnerability. When we openly share our true, inner ugly challenges, we face the possibility of being ostracized.

On the other hand, vulnerability can be a beautiful, freeing thing. When your friends come into your house and you have dirty dishes in the sink, messy laundry on the floor, and muddy dog prints on the carpet, they are seeing life as it really is. Some people gasp at the thought of others viewing their house in such disarray. These same people often gasp at the thought of others seeing their lives in such disarray, but it is the truth.

When we are vulnerable, we are stating that we recognize we are imperfect and flawed, in both deeds and thoughts.

While some people see vulnerability as a weakness, the Bible states it is our strength. In 2 Corinthians 12:9-11, Paul boasted about his weaknesses and vulnerabilities. He wrote,

> [The Lord] said to me, "My grace is sufficient for you, for my power is made perfect in weakness." Therefore I will boast all the more gladly about my weaknesses, so that Christ's power may rest on me. That is why, for Christ's sake, I delight in weaknesses, in insults, in hardships, in persecutions, in difficulties. For when I am weak, then I am strong (NIV).

For when I am vulnerable, then I am strong. Not in my own strength, but in the Lord's.

The Pharisees were anything but authentic, transparent, or vulnerable. They took pride in their position and power, and it was their pride that kept them from seeing Jesus as the prophesied Savior. Likewise, it's often our pride that keeps us from being vulnerable with the people around us.

If you ask someone how they are doing, most people will respond with a quick, "I'm good." But that's not really the case, is it? That's just a habitual response. When was the last time someone *really* told you how they were doing? When was the last time someone told you how the busyness of life had them overwhelmed, how the blow-up fight with their spouse was crippling, or how they were struggling to find hope for their marriage? When was the last time you were really honest about how you were?

As believers, we should be modeling this behavior. We should share our struggles, insecurities, and fears with others so that they can gain the freedom to do the same. Most people assume others really don't want to know or don't have the time. It's sad when we get so used to the formalities that we don't even think about responding with a bit of vulnerability, expressing our desire to connect at the deeper level. It's sad when we don't trust that His love and acceptance is enough, even if those around us don't know how to respond. It can be awkward at first, but if you are around true friends, it is worth the risk.

What if people really knew you downed a carton of ice cream to deal with stress, you yelled at your children to hurry up, and you almost walked out on your husband the other night? What if they knew how jealous you are over your sister's amazing body and your neighbor's swimming pool? What if someone knew how much you spend on Amazon in a given month?

One of the great secrets of the Christian faith is that our flaws and failures don't keep us from Christ—they draw us to Him. Our weakness and dependency become our greatest sources of strength because in them we realize our need for Him, His abundance, His grace, and His sufficiency.

You can be authentic without being vulnerable or transparent. You can be transparent without being authentic or vulnerable. But you can't be vulnerable without being authentic and transparent. So a good reminder is:

Be authentic with all, transparent with some, and vulnerable with a few.

It's important to have guardrails and boundaries on how we bare our souls. It's wise to share more with those trusted friends who are committed to us, have our best interests in mind, will pray for us, and will provide godly, biblical counsel. It's not wise to share everything on social media or with those who only respond with emotions and opinions. This is a recipe for disaster.

> Our flaws and failures don't keep us from Christ—they draw us to Him.

And remember, there will be times to be quiet. There is wisdom in purposeful silence. Sometimes we need to talk to the Lord first. This intentional withdrawal should stem from a heart seeking the privacy to heal, not hide. Lysa TerKeurst has said, "Secrecy is for the purpose of hiding...Privacy is...for the purpose of healing."[1]

Vulnerability is a gift. It's grace-language for the soul. A soul is fully known when it is vulnerable with God and with those He has entrusted to us to live alongside.

So don't be shy, be prudent. Don't be protected, be thoughtful. Don't be fearful, be prayerful. Don't be guarded, be guided. Don't be a coward, be considerate. Don't conform, confide. Don't be concealed, be compassionate.

BEYOND VULNERABILITY

Authenticity, vulnerability, and transparency are applauded and esteemed in the Christian space. It's become trendy to share our stories and failures. But many stop there. They leave out the part that restores our relationship with the Creator and refreshes our soul: repentance.

I hear women all the time refer to themselves as a "mess." And you probably are. I am too. I clearly need Jesus. Just ask my kids or my husband or my extended family or that poor barista at whom I just scowled.

I'm easily angered, quick to criticize, and too often ungrateful. I'm grumpy and I'm selfish.

I like comfort. I like control. I worry when I should trust. And I trust when I should be concerned.

I'm not only a mess, but I'm a hot mess in desperate need of some grace.

But this isn't a badge of honor. We need to move beyond authenticity and transparency and allow God to transform us from the inside out. We need to rest, bask, and be astounded by grace, but most importantly, we need to be changed by it.

We can't settle with authenticity or relatability. It's good to keep it real, and it's great to be relatable, but true growth happens when we change our ways through the power of Christ.

When the woman caught in adultery was brought to Jesus, she was forgiven. But—and we often leave out this part—He then told her to go sin no more. He told her to change her ways. His grace and forgiveness were meant to refresh her *and* redirect her. Grace should transform us so we are compelled to leave the sins and destructive habits that tear us down.

Grace is not soft. It's radical. It changes motives, responses, and purposes. It takes fishermen and makes them disciples; it takes prostitutes and makes them prophets; it takes moms and makes them mountain movers. The power that raised Christ from the dead is the same power that resides in us and desires to remake us.

After we have learned how to be authentic, transparent, and vulnerable, we have to learn how to repent. Confession is not the same thing as repentance, and sincerity is not a virtue on its own. When we admit that we have sinned *and* turn from our evil ways, then the Savior can work in us. *That* is bold. *That* takes courage. *That* invites real life change.

In our postmodern culture, it is acceptable to tolerate all, tell all, and be applauded for the bravery of admittance. But it sparks no change in our lives. Vulnerability can't replace repentance, but it can be the avenue for repentance. The ultimate goal is intimacy with God, and repentance reestablishes it. It's good to admit our failures, but we need to emphasize the turning away from sin and the Holy Spirit's ability to rebuild our hearts.

We should be a community of people *more interested in changing things than just admitting things.*

The reason I like garage sales is because old things seem new again. We not only declutter our homes, but we change our homes as well. And God does the same with our hearts. He doesn't demand perfection; He gives it. He lovingly removes the destructive sins that suffocate our soul. He exposes our need for Him. He places *His perfection* upon us so that we can be safely vulnerable, free to repent and be restored.

The best part is that all of this doesn't even cost a dollar. It is a free gift of God, for all who are willing to spend time with Him.

12

Chasing Perfect

I am the vine; you are the branches. Those who
remain in me, and I in them, will produce much
fruit. For apart from me you can do nothing.

JOHN 15:5 NLT

recently had an important appointment I was dreading. It wasn't one of those "I kinda don't want to go" things. It was one of those "I'd rather clean dog hair out of the bathtub than go to this meeting" type of things. I was meeting with a fitness trainer and certified nutritionist.

I knew it would be beneficial. And I knew her advice and recommendations would keep me healthy. But I also knew the lifestyle changes and the temporary physical pain would be real.

I used to care deeply about my body, but in an unhealthy way. I cared about how I looked in a two-piece swimsuit and cut-off jean shorts. I cared about the compliments I received from women. I cared about the attention my body garnered from men. I am thankful God has done a work on my heart and transformed my view on physical appearance. I now know that becoming healthy is less about how we look and more about taking care of these precious, life-giving vessels God has given us. Our bodies are temples, and when we properly care for them, God can use us to the best of our capacity, becoming a less exhausted mother, a more physically available spouse, and ultimately, a more functional ambassador for Christ.

Before my scheduled meeting, I sat in my car with a million thoughts running through my head. If only my body were in as good of shape as my mind, since it sprints all day long. I remembered when exercise used to be fun. Back in my twenties, literally nothing hurt, soreness lasted a total of three seconds, and I could eat a dozen donuts for breakfast without the scale budging. But that was 20 years ago. Today, if I stare at a Dunkin' Donuts sign too long, my waistline grows an inch.

Unfortunately, our bodies change as we get older. Exercise and food control take more effort and discipline now. This can be exceptionally challenging since much of our energy is invested in our kids and grown-up responsibilities. Adulting is a real inconvenience at times. And those sugary, caffeinated beverages sound way more appealing than working out.

When I finally made it through the door of the gym, I met my trainer. She was nice enough. After a few pleasantries, she suggested we start with a body scan. I'm sure she could tell by the look in my eyes that I wasn't thrilled with the idea of checking my total body fat. And sure enough, it wasn't pretty. Hibernating polar bears carry less weight in certain areas. I would have bolted for the door, but according to the scan, I probably couldn't have made it.

I was told I needed to commit to an entire lifestyle change. This would include altering the way I eat, the way I work out, and the way I sleep. She said it would require a little sacrifice and an enormous trust in the process. While it didn't sound wonderful, I thought I could do it. And then she said I'd have to eat less queso. That's where she crossed the line.

Long story short, I trusted the trainer and my body began to transform. Left to my own devices, I probably would have ordered a shake from Chick-fil-A after the first workout. But I decided to trust her. Her plan was perfect, and although I didn't see it at first, it took all aspects of my physical and mental health into consideration. By exercising just a little trust and faith, I started to become a new person.

If you picked up this book, it's probably because you are tired of chasing perfect. Pursuing the perfect marriage, the ultimate job, the bestest friends, and the HGTV home has left you exhausted. You want to do something meaningful and lasting, but none of the self-help books or success lists have made a difference. In fact, your soul is more lost than ever.

It's because perfection can't be found in things—it's found in a person, Jesus Christ. He is the perfect that our hearts have been longing for. We can get lost in the minutia, the busyness, and the distractions on our own, but when we find intimacy with our Savior, the rest begins to fall into place.

I've tried my best throughout this book to help you understand that following Christ isn't always easy, but it is simple and always worth it. Like my trainer's workout plan, it just takes a little trust and faith. Your soul will soon begin to find peace. Your life will soon begin to find purpose. It may seem mysterious and paradoxical now, but as you learn to love God more, you'll go from spent to well-spent, from fruitless to fruitful, and from spiritually starving to completely satisfied.

Let's take one more look at what God is trying to reveal to us women...

BEARING FRUIT

A few years ago, I was in California with my family. As we drove down the road, our kids were glued to the windows and awestruck with the trees and all the different kinds of fruits. I love Kansas, but it's not the most temperate climate for growing apples, oranges, peaches, or cherries. It seems these fruits don't like random snowstorms in April.

As we passed different trees, I began to quiz the kids on each of the upcoming trees and which ones they thought were growing. They guessed right nearly 100 percent of the time, except when Rogue would shout out something outlandish like "A Doritos tree!" When I asked how they could tell the difference, Reign said very matter-of-factly, "By their fruit."

That's how a follower of Christ is recognized as well. By her fruit.

Galatians 5:22-23 states that the fruit of the Spirit is love, joy, peace, patience, kindness, goodness, faithfulness, gentleness, and self-control. In other words, a believer who is walking with Christ should be recognized by these different attributes, by this fruit. We won't do it perfectly all the time—which is why we need the forgiving grace provided when Christ died on the cross—but we should orient our lives so that this fruit is visible to a world hungry for meaning.

The daily challenge is how to tell the difference between good fruit and rotten fruit. There was no way for me and my kids to tell if an orange is good by simply driving by, just as there is no way for you to tell if someone is truly loving because they said so. You have to carefully examine the fruit. And the only way to do that is to stop, take your time, and compare the one in front of you with God's perfect design.

Simply stated, the only way you are going to be able to decipher between good fruit and rotten fruit is to immerse yourself in the study of God's Word. When held up against the Word, you will quickly see that good fruit will be aligned with righteousness, God's attributes, and a spirit of humility and grace. Wise discernment is critical, as subtle lies and destructive biblical untruths are creeping into many of the "feel good" messages we read and listen to on social media, books, podcasts, and even within the church. Rotten fruit will be about a person's feelings and opinions, human desires, and anything that needs to be popular and sound nice. Good fruit is *God's* design for our lives—rotten fruit is *our* design for our lives.

In Psalm 1, we see that the "blessed" or "happy" woman is the one who doesn't walk in the advice or path of the wicked. She delights in God's instruction and way, meditating on it day and night. She is like a tree planted beside flowing streams that "yields its fruit" (verse 3) in its season and whose leaf does not whither. Whatever she does prospers.

When we remain next to God, next to the source of flowing, endless streams of water, planted and firmly fixed, our souls will thrive and flourish, even in seasons of drought, even when life is difficult and nothing seems to be going well. Life will not always go perfectly, but our souls will be well in the midst of it.

But here's the twist: to produce much fruit, we have to die to ourselves. We have to stop chasing after everything the world chases after. In John 12:24, Jesus stated, "Truly I tell you, unless a grain of wheat falls to the ground and dies, it remains by itself. But if it dies, it produces much fruit" (csb).

To produce the fruit you really want in your life, you are going to have to die to yourself. Die to your selfish ambitions. Die to your people pleasing. Die to your own concocted version of success. If you really want to be like Christ, you have to die like Christ—so He can come and indwell in your place and produce much fruit.

The purpose and peace you desire cannot be attained by your own accord. You need Christ's supernatural power and His presence. Then you will bear much good fruit.

WELL SPENT

You may have started this book with the assumption that being spent is a bad thing, that our struggle is related to the chaos in our daily lives. If so, you were probably hoping I would give you tips and tricks to stop all of the busyness. Perhaps sprinkle in a little scripture from time to time for good measure. And in doing so, you would finally have peace.

Sorry to disappoint you.

Instead, we've taken a step back to see things through God's perspective and the Word of Truth. It has helped us come to the realization that we are spent on the wrong things, striving after the wrong things. We are trying to become better versions of ourselves, forgetting that God isn't asking for perfect success but perfect surrender. We have focused on everything but God. So instead of being exhausted in a satisfied and purposeful way, we are just worn out. We are tired. We want to quit.

But...

When we spend ourselves in the way of Christ, the way of grace, established in rhythms that direct our souls toward what they were intended, we will find ourselves not only sustained but empowered.

When I was a physical therapist, I would often inform my patients that in order to become stronger, they would have to work through the brokenness. They would need to endure exercise that would initially stress their bones and muscles. But in the end, that exercise would be vital to their recovery.

Our bodies have a tremendous capacity to heal. In the physical therapy world, there is a concept referred to as Wolff's law. It is the understanding that muscles and bones become stronger in direct proportion to the stress placed on them. The more stress, the stronger the muscle. The less stress, the weaker the muscle.

Wolff's law could be a biblical concept as well. When we are poured out, broken, and stressed for the cause of Christ, God strengthens us accordingly. He teaches our minds, encourages our hearts, and refreshes our bodies in direct proportion to the stress placed on us.

As we are spent, He will restore.

Being well spent starts with seeing life through an eternal lens and within a different economy. It sees the weak as strong and the last as first. It loves its enemies as well as its friends with a crazy, rare love that is confusing to the world. It seeks holiness over hustle and surrendered sacrifice over selfish ambition.

When we are well spent, we work *from* a position of acceptance, not *for* a position of acceptance. *From* victory, not *for* victory. We will still be poured out, but we will not be exhausted. Our souls will be anchored in faith and transformed by the gospel.

We've been tired because we are constantly preoccupied with what other people think about us. We fret over awkward conversations and unmet expectations. We are constantly trying to determine how others will respond or engage, whether they approve of our hair, clothes, or home. We worry about measuring up and overanalyze every situation, every word, and every motive of others. We are constantly thinking about us.

A well-spent life is one of surrendered effort. It is one that gives 100 percent to kingdom work while resting in the outcome at the same time. One day God will not say, "Well done, good and faithful speaker, author, leader, CEO, entrepreneur, mogul." He will say, "Well done, good and faithful *servant*" (Matthew 25:23).

Live with that in mind. And live like you believe it.

ACTIVE REST

Malcolm Gladwell, the bestselling author of *The Tipping Point* and *David and Goliath*, has an extremely interesting podcast called Revisionist History. In each of the episodes, he unpacks different stories and challenges the listener to examine the parts that are overlooked and misunderstood. His premise is that things are not always what they seem.

The journey of becoming a godly woman is often overlooked and misunderstood. Things are not always what they seem.

Perhaps we make ourselves big by making ourselves small. Maybe rolling around in the grass with the kids, ignoring the lights on our mobile phones, making a family dinner, or snuggling with our spouses is the most miraculous thing we can do today. The simple, obedient life can often be the most significant. Not everything that needs to get done should be on a to-do list.

The quiet life of daily, sacrificial obedience has eternal weight. A fruitful woman is one who empties herself to comfort an elderly woman or a sick child. She prays with the struggling neighbor who is experiencing anxiety. She interrupts her day to sit with a friend whose marriage is falling apart. She may be the tired, young mama, awake at all hours of the night, calming cries and changing diapers. Or she may be the wife who would rather sleep than have sex, but wants to meet the needs of her husband. All of these women are performing sacred work and spiritual worship of God. The world may not see it, but they are as obedient as the missionary in the slums of India. They live out the gospel with their lives.

There are no trophies for these invisible heroes who give their lives and spend themselves for the sake of others. But there are crowns. The most remarkable women I know have exchanged the accolades of this world for a crown that will be bestowed on the other side of eternity.

What is most overlooked and misunderstood is that God is calling us to active rest. On most occasions, He wants our minds and bodies actively pursuing kingdom work while our hearts and souls are at rest. It's a strange but powerful dichotomy that unlocks our true potential while aligning us with the Savior.

The Sabbath is a good time to engage in active rest. Instead of being a day where we can accomplish extra work or try to get ahead, the day allows us to trust that God will come through for us and provide while we focus on Him. Some confuse the Sabbath as a day to kick up your feet and watch football or a movie. It's not merely a day for leisure, but a God-given opportunity to pause and refocus. Not to quit, but to refuel. Not to go numb, but to reignite. The Sabbath is a day to trust that when we pause, He will still provide.

In chasing after perfect, we often confuse the concept of active rest.

We confuse comfort for peace. Our souls were made for peace, but that doesn't mean our lives will always be comfortable. In fact, following Christ and pursuing a holy life can be unpredictable, uncontrollable, and full of inconveniences. Paul, Peter, Stephen, and myriads of faithful disciples have lived tough lives and died for the gospel. But all of them—every single one—had inner contentment and peace while on the rough road.

We confuse striving for worth. Too often we try to be and do all the things, which leaves us exhausted. Because of the pressure from society, we believe that if our actions aren't visible, calculable, or postable, we aren't doing enough. But our worth is not determined by our actions—our worth resides in our relationship with Christ. Our identity is found in Christ alone.

We confuse success for significance. Nothing is inherently wrong with running a company, leading a ministry, writing a book, or being an influencer. But these roles and the resources that often come with them should never be the end goal. They should be platforms so that others can come to know and meet Jesus. The significance we desire should be calculated in eternity, not in bank accounts, awards, or notoriety on earth.

If you find yourself confused and potentially chasing after perfection in cheap substitutes, ask yourself if words like *patience, humility, resolve, sacrifice, surrender,* or *peace* are accurate descriptions of your soul. If so, you may be exhibiting active rest. If the words *restless, urgent, controlling, anxious,* and *weary* are more accurate descriptions, then you may be pursuing success on your own.

Remember, just because some work is invisible doesn't make it insignificant. There will certainly be responsibilities that seem monotonous and unimportant. And we will have days that feel pointless and unglamorous. But we can find active rest in Christ as we pursue the purpose God has laid out before us.

LOVING GOD MORE

My hope for writing this book was that we would all learn to love God more. As women, we are often so distracted, chasing after so many meaningless things, that we miss the joy and hope that is right in front of us in a relationship with Jesus.

I don't often love God more than I love my lattes, my online shopping, my Christmas decorations, my golden doodle, and my kids. Too frequently God comes after all that. So this dialogue we've been having is as much for me as anyone else.

When I'm feeling discouraged, I often find hope in Jeremiah 29:13. The Lord promises, "You will seek me and find me, when you seek me with all your heart."

I don't think I'm very intelligent or gifted, but if all I have to do is focus on Christ and seek Him with all my heart, I can do that. I can plant myself next to the well of life, let my roots grow deep, and allow the living water to refresh my soul. If all I have to do is respond to His strength and direction, I can do that. And you can too.

If you were at the end of your proverbial rope when you picked up this book, I pray this is a fresh start for you. It may mean you need to own your sins and rebuild the relationship with your husband. It may mean you need to quit the job you have so that you can focus on your family and your true purpose. It may mean you need to volunteer to help at the abused women's shelter. It may mean you need to devise a better plan for parenting your kids. I don't know what the specific action step may be for you, but I do know it all starts with your relationship with Christ. Without this foundation, you have nothing.

If you feel both excited and flustered at the same time, let me recommend a few simple steps for you:

Spend time in the Word.

This is foundational. This is your soul anchor. You may not have time to do a deep dive every day, but aim to regularly meet with Jesus for uninterrupted periods of time. Pray for the Holy Spirit to guide you and speak into your heart through the words you read. And be consistent. It may seem awkward at first, but the Lord is faithful to open up your spiritual eyes as you walk through Scripture with Him.

Take the time to scuba dive rather than snorkel in the biblical waters. Learn the context of scriptures. Look for repeated words, structure, and themes. Underline them. Interpret the text within the context of history and literature. Look up commentary and cross-referenced scriptures. Interpret scripture with other scripture. Find a plan and stick to it, even if you get behind.

Let God lead you. It's not a race. Find a tool to guide you in observing the Scripture, interpreting it, and applying it. I've found that keeping a journal or writing down what God is teaching me helps me slow down and reflect.

Find quiet and undistracted time. This may mean you need to get up earlier. It may mean you take the time when your baby naps, your kids are at sports practice, or your husband is working on the yard. There is always time; you just have to prioritize. Don't let the desire for the ideal devotional setting keep you from diving in. The important thing is that you open the Bible and start reading.

When you start to realize there is nothing more important than being in the Word every day and seeing life through God's eyes, things will change. *You* will change.

Pray.

When the disciples saw all the miracles Jesus was performing and all the lives that were changed, they asked Him to teach them how to pray. They connected His power to His prayer life. They realized that prayer changes things.

The same can still be said today. Prayer changes things. It sounds so simple, but it can be the hardest thing to do because it takes faith. It takes faith that God hears and actually cares. It takes faith that He will respond. One thing I've learned about prayer is this—prayer often has more to do with God changing my heart than Him granting my requests.

> Prayer has more to do with God changing my heart than Him granting my requests.

Prayer is more than an effective tool. We get to summon heaven to move on earth. We get to communicate with the Creator of the universe and the Lover of our souls. There's no better use of our time. The pause and pray will accomplish way more than the hurry and hustle.

Pray throughout the day, but also dedicate regular times to go off and spend extended time in prayer. Write down your requests in a journal or put them in a prayer jar to remember how He has answered them. This will strengthen your faith.

Connect with godly friends.

You can't do this alone. We all need other godly women around us, encouraging and challenging us. Instead of getting together to gossip about the latest events, we should intentionally gather with one another for the purpose of encouragement, spiritual counsel, and prayer. We are a provision for each other and a tool God will use to strengthen, affirm, and convict us.

Practice authenticity with everyone, transparency with some, and vulnerability with a few. You don't need a large group of women who know every aspect of your life, but you do need a few who are willing to speak truth to you, regardless of the circumstances. If we can learn to be real, open to refinement, and willing to bring things into the light, we will start to heal brokenness and remove the strongholds of sin that keep us exhausted and confused.

God already loves you. In fact, He loves you more than you could ever hope or imagine. I hope practicing these disciplines will allow you to reciprocate and love Him more as well.

CHASING PERFECT

Most of us have been chasing the perfect body weight, the perfect spouse, the perfect job, and the perfect life. We've looked far and wide, taking advice from moms, friends, and Oprah, yet we still have this aching emptiness inside. We sense we are *made for something* better, but we're not sure where to start.

The mistake we've made is thinking better means perfect satisfaction can be found in a new object or fresh experience But perfection can only be found in the perfect person, Jesus Christ. You may find temporary enjoyment in a cute dress, a spa day, or a bigger paycheck, but the lasting peace and purpose you desire can only be found at the foot of the cross. The good news is this: Jesus is enough. Knowing your exhausting daily pursuits would never reach to heaven, He made another way by sacrificing His life to pay for your sin. And now He waits for you to confess, repent, and turn to Him. When you do, He gives you grace, and His grace makes you perfect.

When Jesus commanded you to be perfect as the Father is perfect, He wasn't encouraging you to find your worth and purpose through your own exhausting efforts. He was asking you to pursue and commit to Him, and with the empowering help of the Holy Spirit, live a life of excellence and holiness. Hebrews 12:1-3 states, "Therefore, since we are surrounded by so great a cloud of witnesses, let us lay aside every weight, and sin which clings so closely, and let us run with endurance the race that is set before us, looking to Jesus, the founder and perfecter of our faith…so that you may not grow weary or fainthearted." He was encouraging you to chase Perfect. As we said at the very beginning of the book,

You can eat all the kale,
buy all the things,
lift all the weights,
take all the trips,
trash all that doesn't spark joy,
wash your face and hustle like mad,
but if you don't rest your soul in Jesus,
you'll never find peace and purpose.

Even though this book is coming to an end, this is just the beginning of your exciting journey with the Savior. You will have good days and you will have bad days. You will experience both laughter and tears. Your life will be stretched and your soul will be stilled.

You've chased perfection, peace, and purpose in every other way imaginable. Will you now chase Jesus?

Notes

Chapter 1

1. "About Gracia," accessed March 11, 2020, https://graciaburnham.org.

Chapter 2

1. Jeff Maples, "Former Megachurch Pastor Renounces Faith on Instagram and Twitter," *Reformation Charlotte*, May 2, 2019, https://reformationcharlotte.org/2019/05/02/former-megachurch-pastor-renounces-faith-on-instagram-and-twitter/.

2. Todd Wagner (@wordsfromwags), "Feelings are real but they are not reliable," Twitter, November 28, 2012, 12:41 p.m., twitter.com/wordsfromwags/status/273889354471047169.

Chapter 3

1. John Piper, *When I Don't Desire God: How to Fight for Joy* (Wheaton, IL: Crossway, 2013), 16.

2. John Piper, "The Inner Essence of Worship," *Desiring God*, April 11, 2010, https://www.desiringgod.org/messages/the-inner-essence-of-worship--3.

Chapter 4

1. Jen Wilkin (@jenniferwilkin), "Devotional reading is like chamomile tea—a soothing drink before slumber. No one drinks chamomile tea before going to war. We need stronger drink to combat the world, the flesh and the devil. We need battle cries as well as lullabies. We need the full counsel of Scripture," Twitter, July 31, 2018, 12:11 p.m., https://twitter.com/jenniferwilkin/status/1024372063954448386?lang=en.

Chapter 5

1. Ann Voskamp (@_AnnVoskamo), "Fear can be what we feel—but brave is what we do," Twitter, October 18, 2016, 4:45 p.m., https://twitter.com/annvoskamp/status/788526326680588288?lang=en.

2. Andrew Bonar, *Robert Murray M'Cheyne* (Carlisle, PA: Banner of Truth, 1960), 179.

3. Jim Collins, *Good to Great* (New York: Harper Collins Publishers, 2001), 1.

Chapter 6

1. C.H. Spurgeon, "Christ Is All," Sermon No. 1006, Metropolitan Tabernacle, Newington, Spurgeon Archive, August 20, 1871, https://archive.spurgeon.org/sermons/1006.php.

2. Paul Tripp, *Parenting: 14 Gospel Principals That Can Radically Change Your Family* (Wheaton, IL: Crossway, 2016), 127.

Chapter 7

1. Mark Buchanan, *The Rest of God: Restoring Your Soul by Restoring Sabbath* (Nashville, TN: Thomas Nelson Publishers, 2008), 35.

2. A.W. Tozer, *The Purpose of Man* (Bloomington, MN: Bethany House Publishers, 2009), 28.

Chapter 8

1. J.C. Ryle, *Expository Thoughts on the Gospels: Luke, Volume 2* (Carlisle, PA: Banner of Truth, 1998), 168.

Chapter 9

1. John Ortberg, *Soul Keeping* (Grand Rapids, MI: Zondervan, 2014), 116, 164.

2. C.S. Lewis, *The Weight of Glory* (New York: Harper Collins Publishers, 2015), 26.

3. University of Texas at San Antonio, "Those with Inadequate Access to Food Likely to Suffer from Obesity," *ScienceDaily*, January 23, 2019.

Chapter 10

1. Francis Chan, *Crazy Love: Overwhelmed by a Relentless God* (Colorado Springs, CO: David C. Cook, 2013), 122.

2. Jen Wilkin, *Women of the Word: How to Study the Bible with Both Our Hearts and Minds* (Wheaton, IL: Crossway, 2014), 31.

Chapter 11

1. Emily Hall, "Lysa TerKeurst on Vulnerability and Dealing with Deep Disappointments," crosswalk.com, November 12, 2018, https://www.crosswalk.com/culture/books/lysa-terkeurst-on-vulnerability-and-dealing-with-deep-disappointments.html.

Acknowledgments

It is impossible to express how thankful I am for all of those who have labored alongside me in the writing of this book. I am truly humbled. There is no greater blessing than to share God's liberating truths and play a small part in the building of His incredible kingdom here on earth.

Jason, I am so thankful you have forever chosen to chase Perfect alongside me. Through the tiring process of writing and organizing my thoughts, I have shed many tears and had countless days of doubt. But you kept loving and encouraging me to set my gaze back on the perfection of Jesus. I saw my inadequacies, but you saw my strength, rooted in Christ. Your faithful dedication to me throughout this process makes me all the more thankful for our marriage and imperfect love. I love you always and through everything.

Reign, Sage, and Rogue. Thank you for supporting me, especially on those days when I've been distracted or exhausted. You've been kind enough to allow me to tell your stories, realizing they are not stories of failure or success, but stories of grace. I hope you always know that *you* are my biggest mission and favorite calling. I am and will always be your biggest fan! My prayer is that the message of *Christ's perfection in you* will be engraved in your hearts forever. You are loved unconditionally.

Mom and Dad. I am forever indebted to the rare love and dedication you provided in the spiritually formative years of my youth. You set the foundation for me at a young age, were patient and gracious through my imperfections, and always refocused me on the Lord. Thank you for believing that, through His strength, all things are possible. I hope that message will be conveyed, not only to my own children, but to the many women who will read this book.

Mama Neal. You have always been a living example of quiet and steady faithfulness to the Lord. I hope I become more and more like you through the years.

Papa Neal. I miss you. I can still hear your voice saying, "If you ain't got Jesus, you ain't got nothin'." We are bringing in the sheaves.

Shawna. You inspire me daily. Your sacrifice, love, and weathered faith wreck me. You are a living example of chasing after the perfection of Jesus, especially in the way you love and care for Corban as he struggles with Angelman syndrome. You carry a tremendous weight for your family, but I'm confident it will one day be exchanged for a crown of glory. I cannot wait to see Corban standing next to Christ and clearly saying, "Thank you, Mom, for always chasing after Jesus."

Luke and Ivy. Thank you for having my back and for always cheering me on. I couldn't have done it without your constant support.

Chelsea and Lindsay. You are a gift. I always feel safe to be vulnerable, confess sin, and share the ugly parts of life with you. Thank you for showing grace. Thank you for calling me back when I wander off. Thank you for making me more like Jesus.

Thank you to my incredible editor, Kathleen, and the entire team at Harvest House. You have believed in and supported the message of this book, trusting that God would use it in a culture that shouts a different message. It has been a privilege and joy to work alongside each of you.

And to the Perfect One, the ultimate Purpose and Prince of Peace, Jesus. Thank You for Your sacrifice. Thank You for taking my place. Thank You for giving me words and always taking me deeper, growing my faith, and making me more dependent on You. There is no greater joy. I hope this book will bring glory to Your great name.

About the Author

Alisha Illian lives in Kansas with her *perfect* husband and three *perfect* children. The director of women's ministry at her local church and founder of Women (re)Purposed, she is passionate about equipping women with biblical truth and hope for their day-to-day struggles. Her days are fueled by coffee, salsa, and more importantly, Jesus.

She invites you to join her, along with the thousands of women who comprise the Women (re)Purposed community, for more inspiring content and encouragement. Her social media channel is @alishaillian and her website is www.alishaillian.com.

Bible Versions Used

To learn more about Harvest House books and
to read sample chapters, visit our website:

www.harvesthousepublishers.com

HARVEST HOUSE PUBLISHERS
EUGENE, OREGON